SMEAR

POEMS
FOR
GIRLS

Andrews McMeel Publishing
a division of Andrews McMeel Universal
1130 Walnut Street, Kansas City, Missouri 64106

www.andrewsmcmeel.com

20 21 22 23 24 RR2 10 9 8 7 6 5 4 3 2 1

ISBN: 978-1-5248-5408-9

Library of Congress Control Number: 2019951262

Editor: Greta Bellamacina
Editorial Coordinator: Lucas Wetzel
Production Editor: Elizabeth A. Garcia
Art Director: Tiffany Meairs
Production Manager: Cliff Koehler

ATTENTION: SCHOOLS AND BUSINESSES
Andrews McMeel books are available at quantity discounts with bulk purchase for educational, business, or sales promotional use. For information, please e-mail the Andrews McMeel Publishing Special Sales Department: specialsales@amuniversal.com.

SMEAR

POEMS
FOR
GIRLS

EDITED BY
GRETA BELLAMACINA

Andrews McMeel
PUBLISHING®

SMEAR

LION'S ROAR – Katherine Vermillion   I

OH FOR SOIL, FRESH TURNED –
Katherine Vermillion   2

WHAT A DIFFERENCE A VERB MAKES –
Katherine Vermillion   3

YOUNG GHOSTS – Afshan Shafi   4

GIRL (A SCIENCE) – Afshan Shafi   7

GIRL (MADAME BOVARY DAYS) – Afshan Shafi   9

GIRL (THE KINDNESS OF SPECTATORS) –
Afshan Shafi   II

15TH MAY 2016 – Luisa Le Voguer Couyet   13

M'DEAR – Luisa Le Voguer Couyet   14

HUMAN – Sophie Morrison   15

EMMA – Sophie Morrison   16

PREGNANCY TEST, IF YOU WERE PINK - I'D DO
MY BEST – Bre Graham   17

I, CARRIED ME – Tenishia McSweeney   18

ON MOTHERHOOD – Tenishia McSweeney   19

WALLS – Sophia Carlotta   20

TWO-FACED – Kayleigh Parle   21

BACK THEN – Kayleigh Parle   22

THE TATTOOED WOMEN OF SEOUL –
Octavia Akoulitchev   24

L.A. – Octavia Akoulitchev   25

NIGHTDAY – Lillie Davidson   26

SHADOW – Lillie Davidson   27

GRETA AND ME – Scarlett Sabet   28

SHE SIGHS IN HER PANTHEON DROWNING –
Brit Parks   29

SQUIRMING BLACK LACE – Brit Parks   30

SACRIFICE ANTHEM – Brit Parks   32

TORSO HOOK PRAYER – Brit Parks   33

SLEEPING ICE RAIDS – Brit Parks   34

TOMORROW'S WOMAN – Greta Bellamacina   35

WHOLE WORLD ON YOUR HIPS
(END PERIOD POVERTY) – Greta Bellamacina   37

BODIES – Greta Bellamacina   39

20 WEEKS IN WATER – Greta Bellamacina   41

WHITE CEILINGS – Camille Benett   42

THE PALACE OF DEAD FLOWERS – Camille Benett   43

FAMILY TREE – Camille Benett   44

LOCK THE DOORS – Camille Benett   45

SUPER BOWL TOAST – Mariana Saori Wall   46

FINAL THREAT – Georgina Mascolo   48

WOMAN IN TWO MOVEMENTS – Eleanor Malbon   49

ECCENTRIC SUSIE – Sarah Roselle Khan   50

MOONCHILD – Sarah Roselle Khan   51

A RED MANIFESTO (FOR THE LOST BOYS, GIRLS
AND NB'S) – Sarah Roselle Khan   53

SOMETIMES I CAN BE SUCH A PRINCESS –
Sarah Roselle Khan   54

MY MOTHER – Sofia Mattioli   56

MIDWIVES – Michelle Hillestad   58

SANTA MARIA DEL MAR – Michelle Hillestad   60

SONGS MY ENEMY TAUGHT ME (CANTO) –
Joelle Taylor   62

THE BODY COLONY – Joelle Taylor   71

STELLA, STELLA – Jaclyn Bethany   72

AND YOU SHINE CONTENT – Ana Seferovic   73

WHILE THE WORLD WAS DISAPPEARING WE GREW
AND GREW – Ana Seferovic   78

BOYS AND BRICKS – Brittany Drays   88

NAKED – Brittany Drays   89

WOMAN TO WOMAN – Brittany Drays   90

TOO SERIOUS . . . – Lily Cheifetz-Fong   91

BIG UGLY TATTOO – Suzi Feay   94

THE GOLD COAT – Suzi Feay   95

MESSAGE TO MY TEENAGE SELF – Kirsty Allison   97

ODE TO VENLAFAXINE – Sophie Thompson   100

EPILOGUE EPILOGUE – Sophie Thompson   101

GIRLHOOD, GUNS, AND YOU – Susan Bradley Smith   102

THE TRUE REMAINER – Charlotte Pannell   104

A LADY – Charlotte Pannell   106

THE ARCHITECTURE OF HER HEART –
Miranda Darling ... 107

THE VOICES ARE SHOUTING NOW –
Miranda Darling ... 109

ELITE MEMBERS OF THE MOMENTARIAT –
Rushika Rush ... 111

THE PEN KNIFE – Rushika Rush ... 113

NEW SKIN – Megan Preston Elliott ... 115

PERFUME (IN RESPONSE TO GIL DE RAY'S SONG OF
THE SAME NAME) – Kirsty Allison ... 117

HOW TO CONTOUR – Natalie Theo ... 119

FEARLESS – Bindu Bev ... 120

ON THE NATURE OF LIVING – Adanna Egu ... 121

ON LOSS – Adanna Egu ... 122

R E V O L U T I O N – Ida Thomasdotter ... 123

L I T T L E   G I R L – Ida Thomasdotter ... 125

THE COMMANDMENTS OF WOMAN –
Billie Partridge-Naudeer ... 126

WATCHING YOU ROCK YOUR DAUGHTER TO SLEEP –
Billie Partridge-Naudeer ... 128

WHERE ARE YOU LITTLE GIRL? – Justine Martin ... 130

I FLOSS MY TEETH EVERY NIGHT –
Elizabeth Hadden   131

UNTITLED – Lori Wallace   133

WOMAN COMMITS – Maisie McGregor   134

MORGDEN – Maisie McGregor   135

THE BOYS WHO NEARLY KILLED ME –
Jade Angeles Fitton   136

GOOD MANNERS – Jade Angeles Fitton   138

TOPANGA CANYON – Jade Angeles Fitton   140

PHILOSOPHY HAS ALWAYS BEEN A BOYS CLUB
(WHAT I WISH I HAD BEEN TOLD AFTER FAILING
INTRO TO PHILOSOPHY) – Jacqueline Moulton   142

DOMINION – Eleanor Perry-Smith   145

VICTORY IN RED – Casey Harloe   147

"MY STATUS QUO" – Louise King   148

YOUR RUT – Stacey Cotter Manière   149

SEDIMENT – Amber Singh   150

FOR HER – Sorcha Collister   153

GROWING THROUGH WHISTLES IN THE WIND –
Sorcha Collister   155

TOAST FOR DINNER – Georgie Jesson   157

LEGACY – Miranda Gold 159

TEXTING THE TEENAGE SELF –
Golnoosh Nourpanah 162

BASTARD – Golnoosh Nourpanah 164

DUST – Amy Burgwin 166

MAIDEN, MOTHER, CRONE REVERSED –
Julia Houghton 168

FIRST KISS – Monica Medeiros 170

THIS BODY – Sarah-Jane Lovett 172

I AM A STORM – Roosa Herranen 174

POLLUTION – Roosa Herranen 175

THE NIGHT MY MOTHER DIED – Barbara Polla 176

UNNAMED 1,2,3,4,5,6 – Elle En Kay 178

LION'S ROAR
Katherine Vermillion

I pay currency to the woman with the lion's roar
for she told me that she could teach me to do the same.
She says that all little girls have lions in their stomachs
that deserve to prowl around their spine
and lurk in their irises.

But she's warned me that many a lion has been lost in adolescence,
for the world teaches us to beat them out from our hearts
and replace them with pearls embedded in the skin,
to bathe in mild milk baths,
and relish the sweet bite of honey on our tongues.

She says they try to wash us pure and imbue sweetness,
stifling our inner beast in the process,
pressing them so far from our minds
that we forget we ever had them at all.

I only pay currency to the woman with the lion's roar
so she can teach me how to open my throat
and let the echoes of fierce felines arch their way across my tongue,
so that I never lose the feeling in my stomach
that power snaps across my skin like electricity.

OH FOR SOIL, FRESH TURNED
Katherine Vermillion

grow yourself a girl, they say
fold seeds into the soil
water them at the right time every day
and out will twirl a woman,
once they laid fertilizer
where her feet would be plucked from the earth,
a sweet liquid of crushed pearls and a drop of mother's milk
to make their girls grow more demure,
ones who would make you brush the dirt from their skin
before they settled themselves down into domesticity,
but the fertilizer has been forgotten
the twining of vines that become a body
allowed to ply the ground with their own tendrils
refusing to be clipped back into submission,
and so, the girl that emerges in the back garden
shakes pill bugs from her hair
as she refuses to listen to the purpose
you say she's meant to fulfil, that she was grown for,
she's a dandelion
and when the wind shakes her limbs
she leaves on the breeze
for a garden of her own choosing

WHAT A DIFFERENCE A VERB MAKES
Katherine Vermillion

men are born verbs
actions stitched under their skin
from the moment the doctor breathes the word "boy,"

girls are born nouns
a name to be called
a body to be coveted

boys need not wonder at movement
their bodies tuned to it
the first time their mouth opens to scream

but girls, so long taught to be a single thing,
stand rigid in their naming
in the place that's settled 'round their throat
tied with ruby thread before they ever thought to grow,
have begun to find their place in action

these girls have grown tired of their prison
finally feeling it chafe their skin
until the welts are raw and oozing

they have begun to teach themselves to move,
to act, to become,
strike the iron of their wills
and pluck a verb from the forge's fire

YOUNG GHOSTS
Afshan Shafi

"My cardboard daisies are in bloom again."
Veronica Forrest-Thomson

I-
In order to shelter amongst the Perspex cypresses
of your last dream,
weave lightly amongst the
thoroughfares of your thought-lantern
separate yourself behind compartments of glass
and forage amongst the splinters of
shock-semiotic
finding yourself
pressed between mirrors as fine
as cigarette paper
hands sweetly elongated,
cloud-filled phials,
into a motion for escape.
bear out sequiturs with lambent discipline,
float on swans with their vitreous ruffs,
their cold balance,
their elaborate éclat.
traffick your horror, spectral baggage,
between Andalusia of yore
and various continents forested with
"violet typing-ribbons" on plateaus
of ineluctable gilt.
though fear of drowning still needles—
drifting above the electricity of taste.

II-
"How we need another soul to cling to."
Sylvia Plath

How the bodies in their lampshade weft, descend
past
the snowy cravats of
the arrivistes,

How the light lifts off their prone bodies like the yellow tar
off a snake's patched rib

The debonair wraith waxes;
onyx skull, an armillary of scarlet parakeets, the hands
as if ribboned in whisper or tossing the molt foil-wings
of the whisper concealed in the family attic.
I would trade half the world for the scent of a
Paris-blossom and for a moment
in the skin of a gloried history amongst
the
silver violinists, the dissident linguists.
for what are ghosts for,
their translucencies, piquant sonnets,
little inferences,
if not to fire at the heart
of time
till blood is one with the
pallor of vision.

III-
"I am so rich that I must give myself away."
Egon Schiele

A pen cannot mark that roar/ fluency. it cannot bear to be set
down or prescribed. groves of mahogany chanterelles. the soft
preposterous clime of Normandy. For all this bereft urgency.
a fisherman's drawl. ruby lagoons. as if the whole outcrop set in
electrum. transistor wires bedeck a stuttering canopy. a frigate
through opaline waters. abalone knees. flagrant tonic gaze. His
women do not smile. neither midnight nor acid rain. raspberry
cheeks and soles of the feet. skimmers, mist, hammocks.
disillusion as if gifted by the revolutionaries. herders of clouds,
empurpled. to exist. his women do not smile. cyclamen veneer
of the hands. to exist. novelettes of loathing. the material
agnostic is. the matter to dispel is.

GIRL (A SCIENCE)
Afshan Shafi

I intended the world
I intended the exhalation
    that with each movement
 confers
   a curling woodlot
lametta armory,
    Chrysotile to wear in teacups

The world is one purgatorium
   and I another
the thunderbirds speak their viridian Farsi (hexameter)
     explain the strength of their
       slim bitter honing
   it is an undertaking, it is an invention
       it is the stelliferous
   Afghan fox welkin
it is Demeter the
    burlesque skeletal in
    moon-pawed Riviera,

it is a Pharaoh's prayer for
    the espaliered comets
      of his chiefdom
it is everything

and I the calf psalm,
an Olympian, a wader of heaths!

I am a bankrupt baron of industry
    sweetening his chronic exile with

     pills for reduction
I am the dun trident

                    colonising
                          a once liquid thatch of earth
yes
I have been of use to the Auspice,
                          to divine the rumor/plurality
                                        of fate
I have been both fable and doll
                                    a White crow
                                          white plash
coursing over my frost palanquin

After all the flesh is only little

                    (Little flesh,
                              but peroration, peroration)
I must keep the company of chemists
                          the bile gurglers
I must not listen to this illness
                    that disgusts the astronaut, the charioteer-
love

          and makes of the matutinal a pale grass,
                peroxide fodder

GIRL (MADAME BOVARY DAYS)
Afshan Shafi

All the good things;
   easy larceny, yes stardust, yes Camembert
yes rafts on Camelot.
    In lichen envelopes
     square cards enclosing one word;
      "Normal"
 silly private catastrophe
a muchness deserving
   Inspectors in cranberry parachutes
proclaiming felony on ground

The whole world polices
   the downy breast of the obscene bird
  (a parturiating Pluto-bound being)

If only I could be - What wonder in composing
     an apathy-ritual
an arietta; adultery
   I suppose I am a
stranger to these pavements (vichyssoise)
    brioche coppices and puddles where haddock
asphyxiate
I am a stranger to appetite,
   My bones (Arabian coda, under
      the clarity of
frommage pastures)

All November, I sat with my wings scaled,
    for someone to come claim me
and yes, to tear the soiled airfoils
    to maculate, torch or deny
   the orality of the wings
When will I cross with thirst

                    a Crimea
beyond the milk bluffs,
When will I cross with thirst,
that
            bloody
                        glacé Everest

GIRL (THE KINDNESS OF SPECTATORS)
Afshan Shafi

Oh no yes
I elude the siren
        her tea-stained heart and tea-stained hair
     the salt of her
bergamot ankle
her lightness-
      contrapuntal
a black garter beneath a
     white burka

She whispers
"sacrifice"
     like it's a Tintoretto
           defiled by a hot-pink pantoum
   like it's pop art
     is holy, is bullion, is fruit.
The
       heavy canoe of her body
procures its swain
      by gumption alone,
   though
     More than anything I want to believe
in other women
       but my throat with honey mintage
    grows like tar over the magi
their clinquant
    thrones
Even the stars are womanly tonight
and I,
    padre, oligarch, balladeer-

add treason to my convictions
and one
platinum thorn-
                    the poverty of being
seen

15TH MAY 2016
Luisa Le Voguer Couyet

I am just a body. Just a vessel. Just a shell.
An empty cavern for you to fill your ego with.
It isn't me - any other would do -
any unimposing absorbent sponge
of sensitivity would suffice.
I am just a shape here
filling in the silence,
a thing that breathes
with warm flesh
to make you feel less alone.

For what?
Ask yourself, for what?

I'm freezing in this body,
a cause worth living for
is worth dying for.

You asked me to come to spectate.
How am I feeling?
I feel fine, always.

M'DEAR
Luisa Le Voguer Couyet

They called me "m'dear," in their northern accents, in his
northern home in the town I now lived. We had left in the
middle of the night, seeking sanctuary from the murky past
we now shared. Problems lay with passions, as blood
mingles with blood through the sanctity of our marriage
bed. Every decision, regardless of importance, pointed us
towards the direction we now had no choice but to accept.
We arrived as we had left our pervious home, if that was
a fitting description, although I didn't feel anything but
resentment for the place.

HUMAN
Sophie Morrison

I feel like a crow on the railway
tracks but incapable of flight
risking life and wing for
food that doesn't exist
and toilet paper that does
inhumane humanity
that leaves its waste
but nothing fruitful for
those who need the fruit.

no money for food
nothing to feed families
no money for doctors
no attempt to heal our holes
our homes
but plenty to hurt others.
we're affluent enough
to make holes in other
places, other people
making money from
arming those who are
harming ours and using
it in the name of
disarmament.

we have nothing for
the crow on the railway
but spite.
no money for food
but plenty for poison.
the most humane solution.

EMMA
Sophie Morrison

you were a formidable person.
loyal and honest and sometimes
abrupt.
never abrasive but so
straightforward

often too straightforward,
if ever there was such a thing.

I saw so much of you in other people
but so little of others in you

you seemed so

whole.

more than that.
as if there was too
much
of you.

I only wish
I wish
for just a piece of your
strength.
your compassion.

all I feel I kept was your fear.

the understanding that
the world is cruel.
too cruel
for a soul as soft as yours.

PREGNANCY TEST, IF YOU WERE PINK - I'D DO MY BEST
Bre Graham

If I conceived you on these terracotta tiles in Tuscany
I'd have called you Florence, only ever saying your name in whisper

If we had to marry, I would wear Gucci
Short, white and very sheer

Amongst the gold, gilt and gaudy
Heavy lids of black and bulging breasts of curdling cream

And oh you angels of Michelangelo and babies of Botticelli
You would weep for the children wedding children

Broken heels and cheap red wine
Headaches on cobblestone streets they speak

Of stories hundreds of years old
And each terracotta tile has a crack - waiting to be filled.

I, CARRIED ME
Tenishia McSweeney

I drowned in my head today,
got lost in the sand
between my toes, on the
beach where you never fucking carried me.
But falling instead, I dragged
myself through,
resting thoughts on days ahead,
keeping it with me, but dulling
the pain with distraction.

ON MOTHERHOOD
Tenishia McSweeney

Sanctimonious instinctive creative block of thoughts,
words and indeed actions,
Mother Nature turned her face with eyes inflamed on you.

Lofty airs of forgotten dreams flatten you, suppressing your
wild scream with their movement through a whistling kettle,
of black not blue.
She mothers no mothers but only what's hers

Abandoning you now to the devil of your fears and hopelessness.
Even the trees withered and the wind ran away battering you as
it passed.
Who had you become in this empty space, where natural rhythm
and feelings were no more

Languishing in this moment of trying to build
your ego from nothing to prepare for this age-old battle
a responsibility of motherhood.

WALLS
Sophia Carlotta

Tears in a musty alcove
as the magician spins his rockin' blues.
You're still there in that filthy house
doing all the things you usually do.
And I long for the filth, for the shit TV
and the warmth you once showed me.

You built walls
only to protect what's soft and golden.
What's the use of those walls?
Walls that made me build my own,
walls that made hellos goodbyes.

I long for the weight of your hand on my thigh
for the soft of your stomach
for the hum of the hamster's wheel.
And I hate you
lovingly
for that subjunctive affair.

Slowly
you'll leave my head.
Time will make me indifferent.
You'll live your life,
I'll live mine.
And all that could, should and would have been
will be lost to those walls.

TWO-FACED
Kayleigh Parle

Tell me of myself,
In a world filled with unrealistic representations of women
Thrown at me constantly like I am rock rather than flesh,
Tell me of the best parts of myself,
Of the possibilities that lay to be claimed
Tell me why society taught me that they were never mine to take?

Tell me of myself,
In a world that when asked for character, hands me mirrors
When asked for identity, hands me race
When asked for acknowledgement,
Hands me gender, and a seat.
Tell me who I am, tell me who I can be!

If there is something worth knowing, tell me of myself!
Not as someone's daughter, mother, wife; don't define me
according to somebody else.
Does a free woman exist? "Liberation" is so often twisted up
with objectification
Trying to navigate our choices as women feel too burdened
by expectation
I just want to shut the media down! I want to stop praising fake!
Tell me how to be proud in a world that's so synthetically shaped?

Tell me of myself, gently and with heart.
Tell me how to keep myself together with these insecurities
clawing me apart.
Tell me I'm ok. Better yet, tell me that I'm beautiful
Without my makeup in place.
Too often when the makeup's gone, the confidence is also erased
And I'm sick and tired of being two-faced.

BACK THEN
Kayleigh Parle

I was a virgin
And you were writing poems painting me as a whore
Because that was your immature response to not getting any.

I was switched from being idolised to demonised
The classic Madonna/Whore
Calling names to try and control something that isn't you.

A woman's sexuality is her own
But you wouldn't know it from the language you use
Outdated views still take the stage.

When men's egos become enraged
And women try to navigate a man's world
Trying to claim words of hatred as their own.

I don't know what frustrated me more
That the behaviour you attributed to me
Was so drastically untrue

Or that if it were true
You would use it against me.
You're such a hypocrite;

You liked me because I was sexy
But the thought of me having sex with men who weren't you
Turned you cruel
Because you felt entitled to my body,
Because you learn that women owe them a turn
That they deserve sex because they did X, Y and Z

I'm thinking of all the women "slut shamed"
Because they said yes AND because they said no

That fragile, fragile male ego . . .

. . . Isn't women's responsibility.
This society is so fucked up
And I'm so fed up with male entitlement.

Back then, I was a virgin
And you . . . acted like a complete dick, to be honest.
You never hurt me more than that before
And I never let you have the chance to hurt me since then.

THE TATTOOED WOMEN OF SEOUL
Octavia Akoulitchev

My skin is not your skin.
It is not a beast's skin, to be hung, it is
to be stained.
O homo clausus, you are cold, you glimmer,
patina of childproof packaging.

We wretched, open to penetration and seeping, leaking milk,
leaky vessel, exuding menses, erratic,
mercurial
- magnificent -

women:
"It's not a damned spot anymore,
It's a kind of ennoblement, darling."

The sandman fucked Sybil
right over,
but we do not sleep in the dark,
our skin cannot be contained within glass.

We fill the space like vinegar
then ferment and generate the heat of fury,
our ink eddying to
the shades whence we've come.

Pour the pitch in the porches of my ear.
Anoint me.
My essence has changed, I am not ashamed.
I am guilty.

L.A.
Octavia Akoulitchev

Worn down Cadillacs, palm trees
Skaters
Purple bloom

The equilibrium between the breaking sea and
Clunky stillness of our ground-floor flat

Has balanced me

And when I reached you
Standing outside the Santa Monica hostel
That smells like mosquito spray

I show you how my freckles have spread to my
Temples

And as you tilt your head
To get a closer look

I count your breaths,
And picture loving you in years from now,
The summer long since fled.

NIGHTDAY
Lillie Davidson

No tea, no book, no pill will make me sleep.
Trust me, I've tried. I've jammed my eyelids shut
Until the night has come and gone. I weep
As sun appears and sears my eyes, rays jut
Against closed lids and sleepless hours have scarred
My face. Television and my laptop's screen
Trick night to day. The mind is closed and barred
Against relief; an endless, whirring machine.
In slumber all the cogs of life can halt
In lands where clocks will never chime. Respite
Is hand in hand with breaking Time's assault
Upon every moment of each day and night.
I watch the dawn ignite the sky and ache.
I am neither asleep, nor truly awake.

SHADOW
Lillie Davidson

I dance with you as you dance with no one
the floor's flat shrine shifting its lines
tugging at your heels to say
there's a shadow
streaming behind you wherever you go

if only you'd look down
pull me up from the ground
and free me from my cursed life
of being stamped underneath your feet
as you pound on into the lives of people
I'll never get to meet

one bright day you'll clock my shape
and follow the rhythms our bodies make as
we spill over cement horizons together
with me tied to the tip of you
forever

and when you lie flat
I'll shrink to fit the curves
of your silent back
sinking inwards as you swell out
until all that you have is everything I lack

actually
for me
maybe it would be better
for you to spend your life
in a darkened room
where you can be alone
and I can be free.

GRETA AND ME
Scarlett Sabet

Our conversation slipped on so natural
Ease of comfort so beautiful
Mirroring against you
We eyed each other on the red sofa on a Soho afternoon
And let it fall down.
And we mirror each other
In our precocious hunger and fire
And desire, to keep surging forth
And writing, our mouths both so full of words,
Couldn't get to stop talking
And our men
From dust to nobility,
Mine more sainted than most.
And you whispered secret waters of the womb and I
Watched
On and played with the evidence of
Your flesh
His eyes round and blue, going along as you packed
Your words with you.

SHE SIGHS IN HER PANTHEON DROWNING
Brit Parks

She sighs in her pantheon drowning

For me this difficulty is a muse-forth
For me this burning haze is a relief of stone

I keep you fairly close to my arms
I am thinking of a different word than arms

I am dreaming of your lost horns
A donation to me

Your glass ending is living
The objects you made are breathing

What a pleasure never to be captured.

SQUIRMING BLACK LACE
Brit Parks

According to Freud, according to Anne Carson, we all need a
prehistory. And we just repeat it.

If you stretch like a thirsty camel into black lace, it feels
familiar, sometimes is a tired word but there is not yet a new
one for it in this Old English,

Some-times familiar is a slow death.
Some-times familiar is a slow life.

I left them hanging like a mausoleum, as solemn is contained within.
I used to scrap lily limbs into those cutouts, they traversed the world,
And they really did,

They gained holes traipsing through mud farms in woods with
air you couldn't believe,
The trees didn't believe it because it was borrowed.

They tore their hemlines on chickens' houses, I am terrified
of chickens.

That explains the holes, a little, in a coarse bother of a way.

I stood there huffing, in my prehistory, with the remote longing
of him scattered as dust in a desert. I will perpetually wonder
why the desert, I thought he would desire to ember into a
mountain's side. Was it dry and cruel. Was it infinite and
thoughtful. I believed neither.

I think we underestimate the ways they chose to be born. In a
thigh, in a storm, in half.

They sinned and then were sewn back in. They made all the rules so they could have different ways to be born and repent and repeat.

Back to salt and black lace that squirms.

SACRIFICE ANTHEM
Brit Parks

In my helmet of the defense of liberté
Screaming of her lock-up
Screaming at my captor or her captor
In this sad Freud not-needed prayer
Screaming my dull ribs are a milk bath
Screaming on panes of glass, obsessive gluing back
Of the smashed funeral of shards
I am certain if I repair them, I can be repaired
I care nothing for the scars, the evidence
The fishing line dragging off my uncelebrated bones

They criticized my Lazarus in Nevers dreams forasmuchas
I pushed my teeth forward and became silent

It is another game of whose country is whose.
No one's.
Land is not owned. The most incredible myth I know is that
paper and ink make it okay for you to carry them around
and stare at imaginary dirt lines frothing at your
sooty teeth, you won.
A captor also thinks he has won.
A King watching everyone starve thinks this is a victory called
sacrifice.

Sacrifice is an anthem. You could wring it out with 4 million
miles of the ocean and it would sink like a stele French
kissing a dent in stolen rows.

TORSO HOOK PRAYER
Brit Parks

In a grappled hook you broke our hearts,
hardened hard marble is bleeding transparent longing in
interium

There shall be a higher order to push pilgrim's mouth dirt forth
we will tomb a body likeness of their torment
we will tell them prayers are extinct

And then the roses, they are stalking like the devil in a damaged
river he cannot regard as wet
creeping around a mouth of petals their dreams are sacred

A canon is one kind of sepulture
it is also a canon
a designed former light dimming as a reminder of the defense,
we will also make a history out of defense like a goose has coarse
fluff, on hay, over eggs

I did ache at the water, looking for you at the bottom
never willing to admit they took you out
a mouthful of the Seine is a respected resignation

I don't know you and miss you like you are my Father, I have a
lot of dreams about Fathers, they are as fragile as my glass limbs

Perhaps you could cage me in a glass that mourns like marble

SLEEPING ICE RAIDS
Brit Parks

In that plaster field of ice you severed a grapple in torso like a pleasing
quite shattering for an eye, the lie as smooth punished-polished
as the marble giving your dead heart a bath

In that rose foam, every couleur will blush a few mouthes with
a weak constitution
but her eyes
delicate workhorse tumultuous wimps

You insisted a monument, whysoever wasn't Azay dragged and
gutted through the streets
in an endless memorial with more sorries than there is air or nerve gas

In those plaster seams with a finger loaned from a bird, she is
dripping our dust in her chalk
burst tongue in a voice we will never hear, drug the myth that
performs like a soft shrug

her mouth is closed
their mouthes are closed
it is sleeping with her

TOMORROW'S WOMAN
Greta Bellamacina

Tomorrow's woman has seen war in heaven
she is the blue of light before time draws

she has loved all the women she has heard
in a throat hood
behind an eye inhaling rain.

Above the stars that cannot be filmed
stars that are not known as paradise
known for their isolation,

biographers of pain
too full of memory.

Tomorrow's woman is the colour of night
tomorrow's woman is your child
tomorrow's woman is shelter

she is sex
the last shock against death,
sex the last peace
sex that forgets black and white.

She is the first to hold a bird in her hands
and learn of foreign love
and not melt at the idea of difference.

Tomorrow's woman is too fat
she bleeds because she knows what it is to feel
a whole generation on her hips
and still be seen as empty
a dog
a fiction

a miracle danger
an ocean of plastic
a soft dangle vine nothing
a war child,

face on a stand
eyes too close together,
mouth like a rental car
feet crossed
the oven is on.

Tomorrow's woman is your father
and his mother, and his mother, and his mother . . .

She is undammable
a renaissance of marching women
as strong as morning
as fearless as water
a school in the wind lighting.

Hands like stolen trees
stuck up in the fog,
a library card to Jerusalem
only human in waves

a courtyard of scarlet fire
closed so far down into itself.

It's hard to imagine what kind of God could believe
the Dead Sea was female,
it's hard to imagine what kind of God could believe
that you could float on your back like this not drowning.

WHOLE WORLD ON YOUR HIPS
(END PERIOD POVERTY)
Greta Bellamacina

you missed school today
you missed the chance to make a wind horse,

cos you carry the whole world on your hips
a home, a heartbeat demonstration, a monument

and you have no one to carry the womb of a rose
no one to carry your whole world in harvest moons

you missed school today
and lay in an imagined era.

and you turned into a woman without the classroom
staring the blank page of womanhood
to a sender of cold war

cos you worry the whole world in your forever,
an embarrassed cloudburst over a field of lost rivers

and you have no one to turn to
no one to let the worry mist into

You turned into a woman without knowing how to be her
you turned into a woman
who is a hidden library nirvana.

You missed school today
you missed the dance works of wild bird keepers.

you forgot to dream and fell asleep
all your ideas were sacked up to the stars

And the music that drips inside of you still
is the magic of pure new snow.

BODIES
Greta Bellamacina

Renewed skin
never the same trace, fingertip

gentle sketched sunflowers
a weeping sewing machine,

grazing the walls like evening ballads
floating earth balloons.

Your back to me
an uncovered palace wall

your back on me
an ambulance carrying life,

it continues to grow
an invisible history

in the measure of a blues
your own grandmother's address book

a small wonderland
like a house mixed up in embroidery

hands in triangles,
birthing dramatic heights

a trolley of love property
resting rebellion

head-to-wing, in poked ariel fire
an old-world sea bird

skin like war on a stage
a winter field in middle snow dust,

rose-tree midwife of windows
daring you by the glass.

Hair of a horse
over a faded clock,

modern hair like rainfall
hunched blackbird dampness

sun breast isles
burning in its nest.

A new ground level
a coppicing love slouch

refurbishing and refurbishing
the same road.

A continual electrical trail
where love comes to retire

where love comes to suspend
a bewitched symbol

a gentle earth undying
a boat in billowing minds

and on the walk home
the child behind you turns on all the lights

all your ruins move closer to my ruins
a whole country, and we begin.

20 WEEKS IN WATER
Greta Bellamacina

I have felt you drinking back the 20 weeks
like it was a steep haunting
like it was too far for you,

some kind of unnamed holiday
neither a question of bearable sleep
nor locked up water

keeping you closer to me without control.
A tossed violet lineage
washed in synchronised ivy

weeping to the erotica of purple
weeping to the same lake, serenity
which is the size of a football

vanishing back a flat eternity,
non-academic nor sophisticated in this water
in this heatwave of unfinished whiteness

a guest of single answers
with familiar nerves,
drowning out the ungathered, reported twilight

a guest of a woman
smuggling fire,

dressed like broken atmosphere,
puffing a Bunsen burner bouquet.

A guest of a woman
feeling a hundred bathing doves inside of her kickback
devouring everything that sinks.

WHITE CEILINGS
Camille Benett

Muffled screams
Drip down like tears
Through the floorboards
And leave a dirty mark growing
On my white ceilings
I keep repainting.

Heavy footsteps that shake the walls
And upend the picture frames
In the tidy rows
I keep straightening.

We meet on the doorstep
And say hello
Like nothing has happened.

THE PALACE OF DEAD FLOWERS
Camille Benett

I went up once
To the palace of dead flowers
A world of chimney pots
And neighbourhood cats
The tiny wooden ladder
Left red lines on my hands
Like an entry stamp

I belong down here
Where the garden grows wild
The plants all laugh at my efforts
As they try to block out the sky
And that dirty rooftop
With its frowning dead things

But those entry stamp lines
Invisible now
Under black light
They'd still be there

FAMILY TREE
Camille Benett

I don't want to grow old on my own

My plaintive heart
An ancient oak
I'll grow my shoots and keep you in

Shed the old bark
The dead skin
Her banshee spirit will leave a gaping

But I will fill it
With softness, softness

LOCK THE DOORS
Camille Benett

Lock the doors
Draw the blind
Keep yourself safe inside.

Let the dirt build up under
Your fingernails and in your hair.

Let the air
Thin with recycled breath
Sit still in your lungs
And let your heart
Beat down the seconds you've got left.

SUPER BOWL TOAST
Mariana Saori Wall

The dress request was
Black bikini or lingerie
And heels
Victoria's Secret Glam
Hair loose
Nude nails
I arrive and sign my name
Mariana Renteria
Ethnicity Japanese and Mexican
Female
+20
-40
I sit and wait
I was told that for 45 seconds
I would be the most viewed woman in the world
Super Bowl Sunday
We're called into the room
A man in black with thick glasses asks me to undress
Against a white backdrop
There is a tall stool
I think about the best way to sit
And wear my Victoria's Secret glam hair
I'm handed four pieces of toast
with the edges sliced off
The way mothers prepare sandwiches
I state my name
I give my profile and turn to camera
I show the back and front
Of my nude hands
All ten fingers
And then I'm asked to lick the toast
With a Victoria's Secret Glam glance
Say "double western bacon cheeseburger"

Three times in a row
And smear the back of my hand across my face
As if I've dripped ketchup on my chin and cheek
I begin to laugh
First quietly to myself
It could have been mistaken for sexy
But how can a woman take herself seriously
In that room
In that dress
With a mouthful of dry toast
You blew one of the biggest auditions, Mariana
No
I blew Super Bowl Toast

FINAL THREAT
Georgina Mascolo

You hold your leaving,
As a constant threat.
A promised punishment
In your withdrawal.
Your absence a penance
I act out slowly,
Days like beads.
Always wondering
What I had done. This time.
I made silent promises
To try
And do better
Next time.
But no matter the ways
I bent towards you,
Contorting myself,
Flexing always in your direction,
Reaching out with;
A hand, a word, some love,
You slipped further, and farther, away
Until the threat became a fact
That neither of us could change.

WOMAN IN TWO MOVEMENTS
Eleanor Malbon

i. some lies about the woman

    she is built eternal, she is mystic
    stars trace her movements
    fingertips strike dulcimer chords
    her bitch hand will stay

    her selflessness will buoy you
    breast bone fragile
    she is for you
    she will protect you from your shame
    you can see her if you try

ii. some truths about the woman

    she is built eternal, she is mystic
    stars trace her movements
    fingertips strike dulcimer chords
    her bitch hand will stay bleak fantasy

    she stands sharp
    in light hearted concrete walls
    she will welcome you but
    only those who look close
        when they look close
    see the city moving behind her eyes

ECCENTRIC SUSIE
Sarah Roselle Khan

Flamingo smuggled weed
a million stars illuminated
the Labour Day rave
and every night
the north-eastern wind
tried to cause trouble
with Toby Custard the lad
dressed in a cow-print jacket
so content with his supply
of unlimited bliss
clueless that he'd be getting
the chop the next day
and Vega, who just
slept and sat about
with an air and look
that never ceased to say
what's the point?
when Flamingo and I
looked out through
two magnifying moons
we saw our ancestry tree
lanterns filled with
trophies proudly gained
through self-hate
dangling from every branch
we melted the mould
for those plastic trophies
with Love's blazing fire
passionate disdain ignited
within our hearts
and at that moment
our future turned
from grey to golden

MOONCHILD
Sarah Roselle Khan

I fluctuate
in and out
of bad moods

The invisible mask
affixed to my skull
is either
as loose
as the change
in the torn pockets
of every second-
hand jacket I own
or as tight
as the 15 denier
pairs that I wear

I count
1, 3, 7
what an
altruistic ritual
burdensome ceremony
I go through
only to start again
before they've even
had time to dry

Spit out the bad ones
before they stick
to the mind
like baby aliens
on a ceiling

Survive and repeat

For how long
now have I
been living
with this
torturous relief?

A RED MANIFESTO (FOR THE LOST BOYS, GIRLS AND NB'S)
Sarah Roselle Khan

Seek shelter under your shade, the shadow of
which is made up of the darkness and light
found within, as one can't exist without the
other. You'll know what makes up both of these
contrasting shades. My own darkness is through
a fractured foundation and abandonment. My
light is optimism through sisterly love and
imaginative joy. I first felt both when I had no
choice but to yield to my overwhelming capacity
to feel. I used to run around in circles, never
standing still, trying to lose my shadow in the
process. Now I stand under my own shade and
let these shadows, which are sometimes heavy as
iron chains and light as paper aeroplanes, dance
all over me, and in this way acceptance allows
me to release their hold and embrace all that I
am made up of. The reasons for why I am me.
What a waste it is to be ashamed when you can't
change what has been. Be careful about what you
constantly dwell upon, thoughts can act as either
your anchor or your wings. Burn the victim card,
then throw blame into the flames instead of to
the wind. Carry both of these around long
enough and finally they'll poison you and
transform into their cousin - self-pity. It is so
important to acknowledge and move on. The
world will not stop turning or stand still for
anyone. This is a golden lesson.

We are as pure and whole as we are broken and
flawed. We are proof that it is more than
possible to exist with these contradictions and
that is a beautiful thing.

SOMETIMES I CAN BE SUCH A PRINCESS
Sarah Roselle Khan

I was blessed with a few mothers, my
sisters, each selflessly filling a role left
vacant and undone. In darkness, their light
guided me until I reached my own internal
sun.

Javaid, Haroon, Amina, Zorra, Farrah,
Homera, Sohail, Somera - I was not named
like these "exotic" kings and queens, princess
in Hebrew, but no trace of Welsh or
Pakistani.

An exotic mystery
is all I'll ever be
whispered the dandelion
to the bumblebee

Spoilt, shopping sprees. Dad drove taxis,
Farrah saved up for an Audi S3. Wearing
Moschino for kids and secretly smoking
hollow garden twigs. We were innocent
arsonists, spraying fires with aerosols to
bake potatoes in tinfoil. Stealing feather
duster plants from the neighbour's drive.
Breaking into abandoned buildings and
running away from invented ghosts.

Top to tailing in bunk beds. Sliding down
flights of stairs on old mattresses. Traditions
of sunny winters since the strange cold
summer abandonment phase. A Barbie
trade for Paco Rabanne who was on a
special diet nearly all of his 9 lives.

Presents and not just on birthdays. Makeovers
practiced on Javaid and I. Hand-me-downs
and attempted Hepburn fringe mistakes.

I stopped believing in the tooth fairy when a
pile of pennies was under my pillow
instead of the usual 50p but part of me still
believes in a world Haroon said exists inside
oak trees.

MY MOTHER
Sofia Mattioli

Nothing else matters
nothing else does
than

    that moment

    that moment
  when I leave
 my mother

Nothing else matters
nothing else does
than

that girl
covered in tears

that girl
exploding with need

that girl

  My mother.

Just two little girls enclosed by care
Just two little girls taken away

that girl
covered in tears

  that girl

  My mother.

Life all in there
In just

That moment.

    Life all in there
    Inside

    Those tears.

And nothing else matters
nothing else does
than
that little beautiful girl,

My mother.

MIDWIVES
Michelle Hillestad

Woven hair, woven hands
the old craft woven
into our blood fibres.
We hold each other up by
wing, limb, mermaid's tail
DNA stand
and serpent's tongue.
We ate the apple. We are the apple.
Black gnostic nectar
from the chalice they pilgrimage
towards. Sisters.

We ate the fire
in remembrance of Jeanne d'Arc.
We are the fire
in remembrance of Salem.
They tried to burn us but
we danced on their pyres.
And we've feathered up from
ash and ember, levitated
over crumbling systems
with rainbows at our heels.
Showed up to their Pentecost
uninvited.

Do the roots you were born under
still call you home? A hundred previous
hearths, hedges and
brooms over thresholds call.
Do the stars you were born under
sing blood spells to your heart still?
Herbwives, fishwives, midwives.
Aunties, grandmothers, girls

making lace and
catching babies, balms to heal
the devil's work.

We are emissaries
dancing doves over landmines
infidels whispering over
gentle wind to the warmongers
like we mean it. Unveil it
like the earth is our final miracle, the
Amazon our intricate tragedy.
Make love on burning prairies!
Sweet prairies of Anarchy.
Like our blood offering is
a tonic strong enough
to heal our history.

Circle up under
waxing gibbous, midnight expanse.
Cradles full and cups as hands,
wombs keep vigil, perpetuate light.
All of us crones, moms and vestals,
roses, hips, shade and night
oracles of our oceans keep
the old knowing in our genes
and revolution in our
aprons.

SANTA MARIA DEL MAR
Michelle Hillestad

This is loneliness alchemized into
a being.

Saltwater eyes collected for an
ocean home of womb.
Somehow I called down
the constellations
with my longing
and made them into a human,
broken and not celestial

but my heart was filled with
scarab wings and signs
for you, child,
who made sacrifice to the wolf.

Once, in Barcelona
I visited the church of
Santa Maria del Mar

and asked that you arrive
unharmed on the side of the veil.
To her altar I brought my heathenry,
her sanctuary glowed with ruby flames
a thousand red praying eyes

watching us genuflect.
After the final frost

a convulsion of Mesozoic spring
brought you

where fallow ground lay waiting.

My body lay thawing,
bared and waiting for
sorrow.

SONGS MY ENEMY TAUGHT ME (CANTO)
Joelle Taylor

(i)

silence was a song my enemy taught me.

(ii)

1973   I can fit my whole family into my mouth   but I cannot fit
me   inside me   we refugee of economic crisis   we cut power line
we muted mouth of coal mine   we ouroboros dole queue
we seaside hotel   we winter camp in living room   write a song
about me, father   we Christmas   we watchers of soldiers in
ballrooms   we danced around   we dead face   we diggers of
muddy beds   we ticking child

when war comes   let him   be gentle   when war comes   let him
be singing

they say that in the morning there were boot marks across the
board games

(iii)

The bed is cold   my teeth are abandoned buildings   somewhere
there is the smell of something burning   a book. a flag. a letter.

in my room at the top of the seaside hotel   there is a single bed
with a white sheet   I cannot think of anything to write on it
the bed is a slowly developing photograph

here.   us around the dinner table

we are smiling like carved meat.   no one notices   the
daughter is eating herself

here.   you walking home from school

your shadow walks behind you as if ashamed   even trees
whisper about you   you have embarrassed the wind

here. him   here. him   and him

a family portrait   double folding uniforms   ironing their
smiles   catching children delivered from the conveyor belt of
their wives' wombs holding baby up to bare light bulb
to bless   it's okay   they are boys

here.   the stairs

and here, the long corridor you are afraid to walk along.
perhaps it is your-

(iv)

my womb   a war zone after everything is taken   after the
soldiers have left   spitting into palms of hands   after shelves
have been emptied and only sell nothing   after the nothing
gathers in great mountains at the sides of the streets. after the
streets are running with hungry ghosts. after women's skins are
slung from washing lines. after children write their names in
the dust that was once their fathers

I carry war in my womb

this is what happened

someone said my hymen was   a door   behind which rebels
were making plans   they kicked it in   paced the room and
filled their pockets with valuables   my mother's wedding
ring. my first tooth. a bright blue hair bobble. your address.
this.

they wanted to know where I was hidden   I am corner of room
I am crime scene an invaded land an oil-rich country I am
divided equally between nations.

(v)

12 years old there are small bodies washed up on the shores of
my eyes when my photograph is   taken   another girl's
face appears instead of mine

(vi)

there are men seated quietly at municipal Formica desks at the
neck of my womb

*You do not look like your face they say please state the purpose of your visit
did you pack these bags yourself*

my sandbag hips. my barbed wire hill. many will die defending
it. others will drown in the sediment of a trench whose walls are
always caving in.

my cunt is a bomb crater the villagers gather around the edge of
and peer into   sometimes smoke rises from deep within
these are my ghosts   these are messages in a lost language
capture them in jars   display them on suburban mantelpieces
in memes   on t-shirts   I carry a hashtag up the hill   the

soldiers spit silver

(vii)

when impregnated by war   give birth to bullets name them
show   them his scent   the palm of my small right hand is a
creased map to safety   I am stopped at the border   I cannot
remember my name in your language.

my skin a white flag   I am waving skin now.   I am holding
my skin above my head

stop shooting   why is the gun shouting   war is an unexploded
kiss buried   the battle ground is the bedroom   two people
stand in   opposing   trenches   behind sandbag pillows
saying *I love you wrong that's not how you say it this is how you say it.*

my skin is partitioned   this bit is yours   parts of my body
speak different languages. after the war I was colonised   use my
blood to power your generators   dig deep in me for your
gemstones harvest my hair and eyelashes, these
drips
of
words on my chin
and you.   you I give my womb to   feed it well   walk it when
needed

listen at night to its curling song

(viii)

the girl whose eyes are shallow graves beneath suburban patios
goes to school and rows of heavy wooden lidded desks are filled
with the smiling dead. when the world ended nobody noticed
the sun has eaten itself skeleton birds mutter bone songs

her mother and father tell jokes about her everybody laugh the
girl whose eyes are fox holes laugh   the teacher   laugh
children gathered like litter around the stairwell   laugh
the social worker   laugh   the policeman   laugh   the doctor
laugh the psychiatrist giggles

the world ends.

(ix)

I remember how silence was a choir   there's you in the kitchen,
vibrato   there's you at the back of the class, soprano   there's
you walking home, tenor

your solo silences are everywhere.

(x)

this is not what I meant to say   sorry   I can say sorry in
seventeen different languages

I once witnessed my own murder   that's okay

after my death people continued talking to me as though I were

still there after my death people tried to hold me but their
hands passed through my skin after my death I came back to
haunt myself often catching glimpses of my ghost sitting in the
same chair as me speaking through my mouth ahead of me in
the dinner queue my bright blue bobble dancing. just
out of reach in a crowd an

ankle disappearing around a corner

(xi)

when war was teething it rubbed its soft teeth against pavements
and trees and wallpaper and
lovers it refused to let go of my hand in public I lost sight of war
once in the park and its screams were sirens and the wail of
bombs I hit people I love my bombing is imprecise this is
common this is to be expected.

(xii)

in the hospital she lies in bed   she has always lied in bed

they ask her questions and she   focuses   on the spelling of
the answers   she is afraid she
will not get them right she cannot get them right the true
answer is   the wrong answer

(xiii)

they show her children who do want to die   hello ghost
children   they are friendly   there are smaller people

trapped behind the bars of their teeth   here is some food that
will eat you   here is photograph of a girl following small
white crumbs of pills home   here is obituary etched in a
bedpost

in his pockets.   the man with the papercut mouth has a box it
too is small it too is velvet inside the box   mounted at the
centre   is a large tear   collected one   drip   at a time
from all of the children   under   his care   tears are crystal
balls   *if you look closely into it you can see your future* he says   she
leans close   she sees   nothing

(xiv)

when the talking begins the villagers hide in cellars or run in
the shade of trees to the other side of the hill   the girl with the
dugout eyes   watches them leave and stops speaking she
talks to a piece of paper in her hand instead   people queue up
to look at it there are so many peering over her shoulder that
she has to stand on the hill and read it out to everyone   they
clap   they look pleased   she forgets what she is saying

(xv)

for Christmas I give my mother an uncomfortable truth   she
wears it when I visit

(xvi)

the dance of the dead womb   she gives birth to the men who
killed her   sing my bright   sing

my angry sing my red   sing my pearl   sing strata   sing grit
sing filth   sing courage   my
unreturned phone call   my rub   all wrong now   all gone
now

they come to prise it out.

it is a summer morning   the birds have forgotten the words to
their songs

when she awakens she is surrounded by strangers   stranded on
islands of tight white beds   archipelagos strewn across the
ward   she waves   but every stranded woman   is waving to
someone else   who is waving to someone else

                    ships pass and do not see them

(xvii)

later I am dressed in bunting songs are composed to keep my
spirits up   I am given ration books of kisses   three hand-
holdings a month   one dry night a   stone rolled before the
cave
there is never enough to go around   I am alive   I am
growing things   war is over

grown men on street corners cower and wonder at the cracks
cobwebbing their faces   not knowing they are smiles

(xviii)

after the war there was singing   so much   songs   ceremonies
of remembrance   we remember the living   there you are

carve own names into gravestone teeth   this is smile   it
is a wall   after the war we set out to find others and guide
them home   we lit fires in our windows   tapped Morse over
screwed rubble   some rubble tapped back

some rubble grew hands   we pulled on them until we had
uprooted   a forest of women shaking their heads of soil
of shame   brushing silence from their shoulders   thank you,
they said   thank you

we have been waiting   we remember you as a child

THE BODY COLONY
Joelle Taylor

today
you are a colony
you are somewhere off the coast of
a land that does not belong to you.
you are an outpost of the
empire of him
detached from your own land mass
an island lifting
towards the edge of the world.
your children will learn another man's language
will never quite understand everything you say
ask you to repeat
when you whisper tales of your body
that Old Country
and how you used to own everything in it.
you will say:
never let a man build on you, daughter.
take a photograph of who you are now
and bury it.
you will say:
the Emperor is wearing clothes, daughter,
and they are yours.

STELLA, STELLA
Jaclyn Bethany

youth is just a flighting fancy
a missed lesson in my sister's composition book
a pair of torn red tights on the cracked stairs of belle reve
a ribbon wrapping a ponytail flailing in the wind
hair the color of strawberries, lightning ever so sweetly in the
rhyme of summer loves and losses

when autumn comes -
the moment is swept away
like lost time
a feeling that you, my sister, will stay young forever
like the glow of starlight
that never ages
your story will last longer than mine.

AND YOU SHINE CONTENT
Ana Seferovic

The border was an obsessive idea:
Parents trashing maps in the air
Drawing new imaginary borders -

Drunk

Discontinued

Unusable parents

Foraging through wild pop-up flea markets -

The long line of distorted cardboard boxes, stretching for miles,
on which people were selling
Toilet paper
Powdered milk
Canned fish
Prescription drugs, without a prescription
Family jewels
Old fur coats smelling of lavender and sour cabbage rolls

Object invasion, objects that are reproducing, flooding, attacking
and devouring time and meaning

Like a small child amazed by its surroundings
Like a small child that knows every
Leaf shape and every ant trail in their gardens
That is how she was aware of streets and faces

We are all on the streets
Everything is on the streets

There is no privacy in war

(Here they are, the divine creatures, how beautiful she looks,
and that dress of hers!
And that boy of hers! His parents work abroad, he lives alone
They send money, he sniffs glue:
I saw seven of me, with seven keys for seven doors to seven hells
or seven heavens)

She was 15 and it was completely obvious to her
Unresolvably boring
And totally unbearable
The movement of organic processes

Untransparent, unstoppable

She hates her new breasts, her belly, her heavy arms, the stretch
marks, hers

The widest thighs in the world

The large mahogany wardrobe in her parents' bedroom
Handles - the metal eyes that are watching her

Nightmares in sweaty children's heads

(There is always somebody who has seen everything)

She opens the doors and dives into her mother's clothes

Little girl sniffing her absent mother's clothes

(Soft)

Now she takes out 2 for 1 box of chocolate cookies
That somebody sent from somewhere
Sits on the floor and eats

One by one

Does not chew

Faster she swallows

Thinks and forgets, forgets and thinks

Touching her thighs after each mouthful

(Consequences should be ignored)

Wrappers hiding in her pockets

(All evidence should be destroyed)

Breathing and swallowing
Calming pain of this gorge spreading
Penetration of organic matter into organic matter

She hates the body

(One day it will be perfect, just perfect!)

Closes the wardrobe
Throws up in the toilet

(All would be better without sound. Switch it off!)

The autumn was hot

The concrete was heating up, her thighs were her enemies -
sticking to the plastic seats in buses
The sound of her skin flopping
Of her skin peeling off the plastic seat

(The city is a wet metal bucket over my head. Ding, dong!)

The moon was a rounded scarab with golden vibrating wings

The moon was a golden pebble

(That I swallow with the same dedication as I devour
The chocolate from my mother's wardrobe)

Songs about carelessness and freedom: Out, out we will go!

Everything was just one big Now
In which objects were piling up

(Decadence and excess at the end of the century -
20 years later fashion magazines will conclude
Recommending warmly the style: it's this season's must have)

And people were piling up
Who were objects too
And exploding
In this meaty firework:

Dusty shoulder pads, diffuse way of walking
Often in the middle of the road
Half-empty plastic bags in their hands
Fluttering in the wind
Printed with big letters:

I (heart) my country

Nobody's beasties
Unpleasantly imposing intimacy, with their supple and
suspicious eyes

(I wouldn't be surprised if they change into people during the
full moon, not werewolves but weremen)

Boys/Men walking with legs wide apart
Freshly shaven heads

Girls/Women pressed into plastic clothes

(The moment you are a queen, under those lights on that dance floor)

Hair dyed into rusted iron

Lips bright red

(The old one, with scars all over her bare back, is laughing loudly with two soldiers while hanging in between their shoulders: Hey I am not afraid of dicks! No fear of cocks, boys!)

Eyelashes coated in a thick layer of sticky mascara -
The trembling tarantula limbs

(The daylight comes and we don't want to go home)

There is something in the curves and in the firmness of all of those bodies that sings:

We have nothing but this body

And this body is a

Diamond

The pleasure of the shining

(You shine content)

And no it's not easy to be this body

(The crystal lattice)

Tension

WHILE THE WORLD WAS DISAPPEARING WE GREW AND GREW

Ana Seferovic

Look at that big one in white trousers, she is going to buy more
bread. She is hungry, tired, she killed her third lover this week,
she is hiding a pigeon in her shirt, or a black long-haired
guinea pig named Satan!

(Her legs are skinnier than mine)

And look at that fast man in the uniform! That is actually a
woman dressed up as a guy, and she is in love with that big one
She is following her, she will get her, together they will go to the
war and pick up stuff from abandoned houses. They will gather
some money and will be happy in love -

Two girls sitting in a local park, skipping school again

Watching passersby, inventing stories about them

It seemed like the autumn leaves were falling down faster and
more from the vibrations of their laughter

(First time I saw you on a train: coming back from The Science
Museum. You were travelling with your parents.

You looked like the future

The way the future looks like in the posters communicating
regeneration plans: cleaned, in new colours, almost achievable
and yet not present

The parents' confusion at your bubble gum chewing with your
mouth wide opened to the world,

was presenting even more, to the altar of voracious gods, their flaming golden baby)

And then a group of people entered the park with bags

Sacks

Blankets

Dogs

Children

She said:

I can't stand these refugees, look what they are doing with this city!

(Her friend was a refugee, she came with her mother and brother, her father staying in a besieged hospital)

Their eyes met

The moment of understanding

Realisation in which her thoughts became just hers

The moment she will often remember with heaviness and shame

The breaking point

Before and after

She became much older, much bigger

She dived out from inside of herself:

No, I don't think that actually

Not me, I am just repeating what everybody is saying constantly

And they are repeating what is repeated

Yes I know

I don't like "all this" either

Except for you and me

Like there is nobody

And I found you

(You glow at the top of the school staircase)

I don't want to be here

And this wind

Here, the wind is constantly blowing!

There is something in this weak ruthless wind, it plays with people's minds

Do you feel it?

It brings me memories I don't want to have

It brings me cards, each day, one card -

I think I learned how to read them. Today ten of diamonds drifted through the air to me, and that means money baby!

We will get some money

She loved the way she was talking, there was something calm, something motherly, magical about her

They were both fifteen

They were sitting in the park, hours passing

It was boring

It was always boring

Boring, boring, boring

It was ringing in her ears like a tottery tram, going from one shithole to another

From one suburb to another

Through corn and turnip fields

Soggy naked ground

Everything is brown

If it is not concrete, it is brown

They went to a shop

They were stealing

They were stealing every day

Roasted hazelnuts, chocolate bars

Chewing gums

At the exit, security took them to the side demanding them to empty their pockets

The whole shop was screaming at the same time, waving their hands, threatening with the police:

You two are here every day! Shame on you!

Your parents should have spanked you more often!

And you are girls?!

Why are you doing this?

We are refugees, we don't have any money

That was a half-truth

Something that she will perfect later in life, she will become an expert in half-truths

(Lie is an emotion, she thought. At least in her case

Lie is an emotion, lies revolve around somebody who is important, and who needs to be protected from unnecessary information, although, very often, that somebody is the very liar, that is me! The objectivity is drawn from the survival laws, of a human heart in the moments of weakness, and a true belief that the waters strained in the meanders will go back to the right flow. - Gently. To lie is to create privacy, in the moments when a liar thinks that it is absolutely nobody's business what the liar does or how she lives - she is busy with herself and a lie secures a free space, free time - disconnecting the world from the liar's privacy, from the liar's "being alone."

Lie is a fantasy, a story, an art

A liar is flexible and understands much more realities from many that are constantly stretching that word "truth" like old chewing gum scraped from the sole of

a tyrant's boot

Lie is an attempt to control (unpleasant) reality with words - the belief in the power of words

Magic believes the same

Abrakadabra

Poetry as well

Religion - Let there be light, and there was light

Truth is without emotion and overrated. I was always truthfully telling you that I was a scumbag!

Truth is, very often, the last refuge of merciless, unscrupulous scumbags.

That was her final conclusion on that matter, and this - as long as the death does not catch me in a lie.

Naked in death, unresolved accounts wide open profiles on all social networks

(How can you live like that?) My laptops, phones, profiles, they will die before me.

If not, don't read! Believe in me! Believe in us! In the best possible version of us!

As I do believe in that, all the rest are dead ends, crumbs, attempts, all the rest are not important)

They let them go with a mixture of condemnation and pity

The longest steps took them back to the park

(Those long, aimless steps, throughout the last eternal days of childhood. A whistle through the narrow streets, wheels on a bike, lizards soaking up the sun)

Let's find some money!

They went in front of a nearby hotel to ask people, going in and out

Mostly men

(Because men have money)

For some change

Most of them wouldn't acknowledge them at all, like at the time, popular seer-healer, with a big diamond letter R on his lapel

He just slid away from them, almost not touching the ground

He had a show on the national TV

Her neighbor loved his show. She gave her last money for some miracle pig fat. Need will make you believe in anything. She gave her last money to buy herself the ability to look at her husband's needy, ever-sinking eyes. He died after a month, leaving behind him three children and a bucket full of pinkish stale pig fat

Then, a big, muscular guy in a leather jacket emerged from the dark

All sweaty, grinding his teeth, talking loudly

His arms were rowing through this continuous wind like he was
chasing away all the spirits that were entering his nostrils,
mouth, ears, scratching his freshly shaven cheeks:

Women, that is kids! Where are you heading to? I am going to
see my mum, you know that even I have a mother!
And she loves me madly!

Mothers are crazy!

You don't have money ha? This uncle here has money,

dope, speed and a big boner! Joking! I have Coca-Cola! Want it?
Why are you dressed up like that? Has somebody died? Why
don't you put on some flowery miniskirts and stuff?

He started to rummage through his pockets, throwing around
crumpled betting tickets and pumpkin seed shells, muttering in
his stiff chin:

I am out of cash

He looked left and right and showed the direction with his head:

Follow me!

The two of them executed the order like soldiers, and walked
behind him to an off-licence

Resembling two big penguins

He whispered something to the owner, then smiled, so tense as
if his face was going to burst:

The boss says, take what you want!

If you need anything, you know where to find me - he winked

and staggered off across the street

They took a few beers and joined kids in front of the shop

The kids were drinking, smoking, asking for money and listening to a young man, freshly back from the war:

We would empty the missiles and fill them with money, the other side the same but with weed, and we would fire that across the front lines

So we were smoking a lot

I wouldn't know if I killed somebody, you just fire a missile

I am sure I must have

Then the boys started talking about army recruitment and what were the best ways to avoid it: Just say that you are mad or a junky or a gay

The best is to hide

Then some of them started to argue that all of them should go to the war and help their country

At that moment, she drifted away -

Observing her forehead - it was shiny, big, rounded, china moon like

She put her head on her shoulder

The cans were empty

What shall we do tomorrow?

I don't know

Depends what the wind will bring

Probably, nothing again - their laughter - metal coins falling on a pavement, ringing through the hollow night

She touched her face

They were kissing long

While the world was disappearing her lips were soft

While the world was disappearing we grew

And grew.

BOYS AND BRICKS
Brittany Drays

The biggest mistake perhaps is that we tell daughters
That sons are made of bricks
They are strong and secure and they will protect daughters
But we fail to tell daughters that
Bricks can break
And when they fall apart
They will take daughters down with them
And we fail to tell sons that it's okay to break
And we shouldn't scare sons with the weight of a woman
Sons need to know that crumbling
Doesn't make them weak
But sons and daughters should be taught that they are not weight
Meant to push over walls
Sons and daughters should take each other's bricks
And build walls together
And keep those walls
From crumbling
On each other

NAKED
Brittany Drays

You were the first one to see me
Completely naked
You took my guard
And slowly you pulled it down
Throwing it on the floor
You ran your warm hands along years of criticism and never once felt it
It didn't stop you from unbuttoning my insecurities
Sliding them off my shoulders
Exposing my battle wounds that you unclasped and held so gently
You unzipped my every flaw
That I was instructed to cover up
You stripped me of every defense mechanism that I tied on so
tightly
And there I stood
In front of you
Completely naked

WOMAN TO WOMAN
Brittany Drays

I am not here to race against you
I am here to pass you the baton

TOO SERIOUS . . .
Lily Cheifetz-Fong

White, cold bone,
The colour of the Day of the Dead masks hanging on the wall,
Hanging like a visage with nothing behind it,
Nothing to think or to love, like parts of our world,
The masks we buy with gold, shimmering like the only hope left
in a Syrian family's money box,
To me a mask is a small luxury.

Amaryllis red dripping like serene dew drops onto the ravaged
remains of a life,
Ebbing through the cracks like a trickle of water seeps hatred,
A mother desperately trying to gather the remains of a ruined
life and put them back together piece by piece.

My fingers clicked on the lettered keys,
Clinking heavy like a ball and chain,
They said I was too serious to beat their high market,
They said that no-one's fingers would be blackened from the
print of my "seriousness,"
Only after they read what they want to read would they go and gasp,
and wash their dirty fingers from the lying print,
I know they are too scared to face the grim reality; to face the fact
that they are being lied to over and over,
So they lock the room swimming with lies.

My eyes begin to burn,
I know the truth,
I have seen the truth.

I have met the guards who stand like zombies; dead eyes unblinking,
faces emotionless,
And yet the truth prickles all over me,
The truth that problems are ravenous and feed off fear,

The truth that people like me are promoting the creation of
their food;

That people like me are spreading false fear,
Somewhere at the Earth's core there lies an invisible blender
mixing all the world's problems and spitting them out to the
wrong people.

My fingers clank on the gleaming laptop keys,
The keys that have the power to poison the country,
I can hear the sound of a nervous boy shaking like a newborn
deer;
The nervous clicking of the gun in time with the clicking of
my keys.

My world is in a silken shell,
A shell where the outside cannot harm me,

Every time I read my lies out loud I can feel the enamel of the
shell splitting,
I see glimpses of another world,
My eyes sting and like a fist I have to clench them closed once
more,
Again I feel my shell healing but deep down I have found the
key to my soul secret,
I know I am trying to block reality and fall back into fantasy.

I have known the invisible tale woman who stalks around the
room,
I have worked in coalition with her churning out lies and tales,
Her spidery, gnarled fingers have plucked at the keys,
She has leapt inside me and comforted me,
She has persuaded me to not rebel against lies and reassured me
that it is not that bad what I am doing,
That print doesn't lie,
The spidery, gnarled fingers were once mine a long time ago,
Now it is time I stabbed her heartless heart of twisted tales and

false print.

MARMITE CRISIS is more important than children dying
every day as a result of procrastination and hatred?
The tale woman has distorted people's minds,
It's okay for police to be asking a Muslim to take her burkini or
head scarf off but not a nun to take off her habit,
The tale people have spread propaganda from the North Pole to
South America.

Like a print, tale men and women have been duplicated
throughout the globe.
Almost every time a journalist is recruited to work for the press,
a tale man or woman is born,
Therefore, I think there is something I ought to say: I AM A
TALE WOMAN,
Never again are they going to say I'm too truthful to beat their
high market,
Never again are they going to say I need to tell white lies because
you know what,
I RESIGN!

BIG UGLY TATTOO
Suzi Feay

At the water-park in intense July
Kids hose each other down and dare
A path through grey veils of spray,
Scamper across the moulded concrete dish
Splitting and shattering palm tree jets.
Babies sit sudden, heavy, boggled with the din.
Their skin is poignant, buttery. Blank vellum.

Every adult is a spoiled exam paper,
Rough notes towards a personality.
Everywhere I look – big ugly tattoos that announce
I want to be a dragon or a Maori or an ancient Indian sage.
Coordinates. Unicorns. Skeletons playing cards.
Mums with back-fat flex rose trellises no prince will ever climb.
Snakes coil up Krispy Kreme calves. A hot air balloon. A swan.
You've dealt yourself a Tarot card, but it's always the same one.
You've drilled an extravagant cutaneous vow
That you'll always feel exactly the way that you do now
But that flame whose name scrolls your breast loves someone else
And proof of pain's no guarantee of all the rest.

The hook of a drawn wire coat-hanger makes a pun
Of a girl's soft nape and scapular. That joke's not good enough
To outlast the afternoon. I hope it's what it looks like,
Ballpoint pen, to be scrubbed off soon, but I'm not sure
Of anything, not least the name, sign, sigil or seal
That ever would needle outwards from my mind
To print an empty promise on my plain, changeable skin.

THE GOLD COAT
Suzi Feay

Ablaze in my gold coat
With the fur-trimmed hood
Black lining and swanking hem
In the lunchtime pub fringed with
Hanging baskets and hanging men;
It's doing the trick
At the crush of the bar,
Tens and twenties flicked high
Two swells dock right by me
Bobbing and teasing
Fingering the glimmer.
I tell them it's bomb-proof
A shield, a deflection
From the recent blasts
In our packed lunch hours.
The coat has magic powers
For five minutes, while pints
Flash bronze on the counter
And gilded shafts fly.
I'm mile high. Then, serious
They lean in and confide:
In your coat, your gold coat
You make us grin
But it's your friend
We're interested in
The beauty by the window
Glazed in the sun.
We think you're great
But what are our chances?
Spill all you know.
Be a sport, be a pal
Be our tongue, be our eyes.
They don't apologise

And I am not their mate.
I think they are amazed
By what I finally say.

MESSAGE TO MY TEENAGE SELF
Kirsty Allison

You're too fucked to read
You can't see
I hate that about you
Makes your youth a stained dream

Broken virginity

Makes you take more

Your beauty - that green fur coat
They are talking about you

You are different

Careless

Bleeding like fire
Steak in knickers
Your hair is a limoncello abortion waiting to happen
Trembling kidneys, you don't know what a kidney does though,
do you?
You are in the park

Because everyone's doing it
does not mean it's okay
It's not a fashion parade
Look after your clothes, and they look after you.
Your mother knows

You loved him.

When yes means no. After no, and no, and

You know this is going to fuck you up for the next 20 years?

You will never be normal

And you blame him

Victim - don't be one

Your body is freakish

You are not Kate Moss
And never will be

My shell is not yours
You become everything you wanted to be.

They're all automatons on head drugs, and bed drugs - or hamsters
On wheels
Prescribed to keep them
Sharing tips
Like a bag of chips
To boardroomers and slum runners

You scare them with your stinking skunk potency
Rich in spirit, sexual spirit
Bottle it, love
Not yourself
With the sheer ends
Or that was in your 20s
It all blurs

Enjoy sex.
It's okay

Live it
Love it

You're doing it right
All they have is experience
And nothing will teach you that
Only time's whip

Get the tit job the agent told you to get to stay on TV
Or go to Ibiza
As you will

Take that world ticket with a camera for a year
London will not die without you

But no, I'm not sure you should take quite that much
But you are only young
And so pretty
Did he ever tell you that?

ODE TO VENLAFAXINE
Sophie Thompson

Waltzing on the rubble fancy-free debris
Diagnoses a saturnine child
A posy of perils
Lily-pondering in corrosion
Sharper than forget-me-nots
Like how ring a ring a roses is about falling
My dosage increases dullness increases
If I were a colour I'd be beige
And the Northern Line, once lullaby now migraine
Junction damp dripping to chews now tarred beneath shoes smog
This smog big smoke
Fumigating menthol
Take me to cottonwood buttercups neat chins
Glowing can you untangle my hair
Please, it can be such a weighty mess

EPILOGUE EPILOGUE
Sophie Thompson

Be wary of boys with bookshelves weightier than their brevity
Warning sign of a wanderlust tasting tongue
I'm glad you're older than me but I wish I wasn't younger than you.
It's like
sometimes I wish you lived closer and
sometimes I wish you food poisoning.
Tell me I sound like a song
(ink wrists and I'll become one)
Tell me you still like my face and then "I don't want
To be your goddamned Humbert"
Spreading like ivy across your skin and
pressed forget-me-not in dog-eared pages
Tell me I sound like a song
(but you'd written the song for a stranger with a shared name)
But Sal Paradise wouldn't smoke an electronic cigarette
But you've only seen those freckles you so liked four times
But I don't want to be your skin, your soul
Not even your Dolores
Claiming you were a growing pain whilst I was nothing more
Than a writing prompt

GIRLHOOD, GUNS, AND YOU
Susan Bradley Smith

*after Meherun Nesa (1942-1971), poet & martyred Bengali intellectual,
murdered age 29*

1

Today, according to the tabloids, Dhaka is a dysfunctional
megacity. The drains in this mighty capital can't cope with
monsoonal flooding. In the 1960s the city worked, but what
worked for six million people doesn't for seventeen, so I don't
drink the tap water, not even for solidarity. The Chinese have
done a billion-dollar deal for a Dhaka-to-Chattogram high
speed train. The rice crop is set to hit eighteen million tonnes,
above target, yet one-and-a-half million bank accounts have
been closed by unhappy citizens. Everywhere, a crush of hope
and filth.

2

One dark night in March of 1971, Operation Searchlight began
its killing. Nationalism (bad luck) is such a cultural thing,
what with its shouting intellectuals and poets and Language
Movements. Bang bang bang went the Pakistani guns.
Bangladeshi writers and academics were taken blindfolded to
torture cells, then executed. Revolutionaries do not kiss the
enemy. *Kill three million of them and the rest will eat out of your hands.*
Poverty is a flame-shaped harridan, but she was never the main
event.

3

I write to you, dear Meherun Nesa, daughter of the British
Raj, to say sorry. I'm glad the 1960s were good for you, you
trailblazer, copywriter, Philips Radio company girl. The odd
spot of family financial insolvency had not stopped you writing
Bangla poetry for a decade before graduating to mass uprising
participation and hoisting of the Independence flags on your

roof, which sadly led to your murder alongside your mother and
brothers. Still, your murderer was eventually hanged, and a
stamp with your face on it was released. Documentaries were
made. But I don't need to tell you your own pro-liberation story:
our demands must be met. Amader Dabi Mante Hobey.

4
Did you feel your body being chopped into pieces and cubed and
moved, like trying to solve a problematic sestina? Even that is
a PG version of events. Real story goes: bullet in stomach head
bashed on floor raped then gang-raped to death last penetration
being a bayonet skewered body parts thrown from soldier to
soldier (sport). Who can remain steady, knowing this? *Our
demands must be met.* Amader Dabi Mante Hobey. For you,
for this, I will always pray, to that bitch, the moon, who
does nothing.

THE TRUE REMAINER
Charlotte Pannell

It doesn't change
it doesn't change
it doesn't change
it doesn't change

we remain

the material
bone china
or bone idle
made to last
or built for a day
rustling,
old
or only new
only if you knew

we remain

furrows
or furrowed
waved
or tonged
so soft
or so brash

we remain

quiet
or no control

we remain

no injection
no change (believe it)
you wouldn't believe it
until you see it

sweet expectations
bitter mouths

resistant
the water pools elsewhere

Maintain
Maintain
Maintain
we remain

A LADY
Charlotte Pannell

I have a wardrobe from my Nan's,
A gentleman's wardrobe.
My piles of clothes outgrew it
A long, long time ago,
Where is the gentle woman?
Where did we go?

THE ARCHITECTURE OF HER HEART
Miranda Darling

She was love.
Lying on the plastic floor
she felt the tender tug of
a thousand delicate threads
holding her
a myriad of gossamer strings
tethering her to the earth
the hug of the unbreakable web.

She was the soft abyss
the cavern deep
the ocean into which the rivers of silt poured;
she was every hand
that has ever stroked your face
she was nightsong and birdsong
and the velvet touch of forever;

the ever-fraying edges of the world
unmaking and making
the unravelling of every sweater and
the source of all red threads
she was the mountain shoulder to hip
the valley of the waist casting long shadows
over the grass

When they asked her – those voices in that room –
to explain the point of her existence
she could find nothing to say
what word should she choose?

The dust motes hung suspended in her eternity

The task was impossible
and so she began it
the pearl dissolving

THE VOICES ARE SHOUTING NOW
Miranda Darling

The swallows refuse to roost
but insist upon making looping swoops
through the sky
soft and low
feather-tip brushing tussock-tip
over and over they come
one hard on the tail of the next
formation close and tight
dark with single purpose
until that tremor of doubt
runs through the flock
and they scatter upwards
schooling and wheeling
their sharp shapes the only point
of purchase in the sky

The eye slides around
and has no choice but to follow
the movement of the birds
of those enchanters

The air crackles lightly as they settle themselves
now on the ploughed furrows
their beaks taking the occasional jab
at an invisible delight

An exhalation
an intake of air

Until like gunpowder
some subsonic jabbering of the earth
scatters them upwards again
launches them upwards

soft fireworks of brush and feather
exploding outwards now
(it seems forever)
each swallow now alone up there
one flying forever away from the other

The blue will never hold them

ELITE MEMBERS OF THE MOMENTARIAT
Rushika Rush

Behold the fallen woman,
hyper-lashes in smears &
thighs of marbled jelly,
a museum, yet
      some small voice speaks out

restore all processes of change,
sky-born & elemental -
there is nothing to love
about unlined faces,
      unless within motherly hope.

Look in one mirror for decay
yet two for infinity,
an elegant mathematics
- swallow it.
      The world is bigger

than a face, the thousand ships
were ready to launch regardless,
though it must be said that
the curve of her eyebrows obeyed
      The Golden Section.

Notice that exquisite
Japanese face cream
is nothing more than
poetry & dust, you could blush more
      from a song

or from eating printed words,
all demi-plumes plucked
from a Wildean dream,

sordid & complete,
        an ellipse of light.

Page 37, how fasting fires the metabolism –
turns apples to pears,
but disregards the offering of
how mouthfuls of nothing
        bring one closer to heaven

in parabolas and diamonds of projected
daylight. Step by step,
bones grow weightless like wings
spun from a 3D printer
        & mind is a harmony,

but let's face it, who would believe that
without a death sentence?
Can we ever learn
how to experience poetry
        without the presence of ghosts?

Minds rebelling against weak phenomena
& all sewn with hope
about our terminal futures,
we naturally wear
        a burnished glow.

THE PEN KNIFE
Rushika Rush

Why do you want it?
my friends asked.

I just do.

I climbed a tree and
carved the name of the boy
on the train with the fringe.

I used the tiny tweezers
like a doll's surgery to pull out
a rose thorn from my blushing thumb
then sawed a thin twig clean off
the mother branch, leaving an
abrasion of ozone green.

Descending, my fishnets ripped
and I sighed, thinking
about my mother and her lovers.
At the bottom I used
the tiny scissors to cut off both feet
making curious circus leggings.

I want it to gut and clean a fish
I told them.
They flicked their immaculate hair
and puzzled,
Is that poetry? they asked,
Because you're the least practical
of us all.

Maybe I replied.
Or maybe it will make me practical.

Then it's poetry
said my friend, and flicked out
each silver-tongued blade
one by one, admiringly.

NEW SKIN
Megan Preston Elliott

As the years slipped by
Our skin became bound
New layers grew
Closing the gap
Between us

We became
Wrapped
Cocooned
Until I did not know
Where I ended
And you began

I'm not sure you realised,
My love,
That you were a sponge
And I water
Contorting
To fit the shape of you

Until the weight of us became too heavy
And all it took
Was just one more drop of me
For the flood to begin

I burst out
Blind
Into the abyss
Lonely
Shivering

Wading through the flood
I stumbled

And lay still
For a while
Letting the water consume me

Suddenly
Spluttering
I found the strength
To rise to my feet

I trudged on
Whispering your name
Not noticing
The flood was subsiding
Not realising
The skin that once bound us
Was beginning to peel

Raw flesh
I emerged
And I could see,
Finally,
I was free
To grow
A new skin
Of my own

PERFUME (IN RESPONSE TO GIL DE RAY'S SONG OF THE SAME NAME)
Kirsty Allison

I smell you as a memory
Of factory foiled walls
Glimpse your sunken cheeks
Sniff your velvet claw
I thought your scent had left me
But it pulls me to the floor
Past Sports Direct
Beyond social mores

The heat of chasing bondage
Your heavenly boxing glove
Labels don't betray us
This obsession's not love

I touch your head
You stroke my neck
Put my hands behind my back
Undressed invisible
Indivisible
Fond choke
Emulsify me
No betrayal
Floating outlaw.

Rope's in the cellar
Tools in the drawer
I'll sell it all for you now
Whip me, sweet horsetail

This distraction's a one-way street
I'm undermined
You're so hard

Neediness upsets me
Vapor's clear
So near
You never left me
My favourite perfume

HOW TO CONTOUR
Natalie Theo

Hey girl
Why don't you highlight that heart
Like you do your cheeks
Shimmer it up
In five easy sweeps
Contour, contour, show off that mind
Sculpt, sculpt and then define
Brush up with words
That hold true for you
Palettes of passion
Go on try every hue
Wild love is red
Heartache so blue
Black is a hole we all fall through
Blend, blend, smudge it all in
Make those mistakes
Just start over again
Easy on that bronzer
You already glow
Over and over and over you go
Lashing and lashings
A good mascara wand
Open up those eyes to the world beyond
Dazzle for that selfie, girl
Don't forget to wink
Your heart is so much prettier
Than you'll ever think

FEARLESS
Bindu Bev

Sometimes I close my eyes
And I can feel my heart pounding
My ribs a humble drum
To the quick-paced cadence of my
Self
A memoir to the wild
To the hoofed ones whose feet drill into the earth
In grounded flight as they speed across landscapes untouched
Leaving in their wake those soft Indentations in the earth
Signatures of Journey
I see them in my mind's eye as I sit in stillness
And know
That I am never still
That this throbbing in my chest is the reminder that keeps me
With them
Running
Towards the unknown
-Fearless-

ON THE NATURE OF LIVING
Adanna Egu

My hand slips over wet blades of grass.
The sun touches me where you do not,
so I pluck the dipping daisy.
I pick myself.

Light hits my face my back my breasts,
all of this warm, holy flesh.
Feet trample unsullied green

& as I reach towards the sky,
my heart steady drums this ancient chant:

I am.

ON LOSS
Adanna Egu

At seventeen, I have known loss:

she drags behind me,
dirtied silk sewn to my leading
limbs.

She leers from the mirror &
I deliver four swift blows to her jaw;

here is the *crack, crunch* of
bone striking glass.

I didn't always hate her.

In the beginning–
she came gently
(as shadows often do),

lulling me to sleep with
ripe half-truths.

And when the daylight hit my eyes,
I was bare arms and legs,
                    falling.

4,000 miles from where I hit her, she sits on my chest.
I hadn't realized, but some feelings can travel too.

REVOLUTION
Ida Thomasdotter

I watch that sliver
first light
cutting the sky open
to divide the darkness

I feel a cry
curled up tight
halfway up my throat
ready to spring forth

Ready to invoke every spirit in the night
to entice and seduce them all, suck them in
to store them like steel under my skin
just so I can grasp that knife;

They won't need to thicken my blood,
the freer it flows, the harder my resolve
milk, I have none to turn to gall,
but if I did, it could only harden me further still

This Revolution requires real strength,
the kind that comes from inside a person's core: the bloodied walls
of wombs that echo the very bang that breathed life into this soil,
the kind of strength that doesn't shy away from pain
or tears or emotion or blood
but expects them all
like the sky expects there to be weather

This Revolution will claim many lives,
so that a few can persist,
and their blood will not be on our hands;
we only bleed ourselves, and won't stop until we're dry
we won't have time to sleep at all

and those of us that make it through the night
we will watch that sliver of first light
remember every hand that held the knife
and smile

LITTLE GIRL
Ida Thomasdotter

My mind explodes in galaxies I try to contain
the comets and meteorites supernova ideas
that spark another myriad of fragmented thoughts
shooting criss-cross in the peripheral corners of each
dimension of each
room of my mind implodes into quiet fog that ripples
across the water surface of me and you
reach in and pluck a single shell from the bottom
of what I meant to tell you
and then we're diving together except I don't always remember
how to swim
and the beams of sunlight that break
through the dark are too glorious anyway
so why would I ever want to not sink
except my gills aren't gills so much as unsent letters that I meant
to send you
and never did
because I never do
my suitcases and backpacks are stuffed with forgotten letters and
postcards
I have your name under my tongue like a naughty mid-week sweet
like a cyanide pill
I speak to you every day in my mind, still, even as the fog slithers
back in
and I lose sight of myself
and although I never had you I feel like I'm losing you too
and even so
I whisper your name
and wait

THE COMMANDMENTS OF WOMAN
Billie Partridge-Naudeer

For every pound a man makes in the UK, a woman makes around 80p.
That's on average; it doesn't account for the huge disparity in terms of
intersectionality. With that in mind, I've adjusted my workload accordingly.
Here are the 8 commandments.

Thou shalt take great care when propping a leg up on the side of
the bath to get the right angle for sliding the Mooncup in, lest
thou should slip and fall and potentially die with thou's knickers
'round thou's ankles.

Thou shalt STOP BUYING HOUSE PLANTS. You don't even
have anywhere to put this one. It's over, it's done.
They're all dying before your eyes at different rates.
Despite what you think, your flat is not the Garden of Eden,
our lot got marched out of there some time ago
Although, to be honest, if that's the way they want to be about it,
maybe we didn't even want to be in there anyway.

Thou shalt not make brash hair decisions in the midst of a
depressive episode. No, you would NOT look good with hair
like Natalie Portman in "Léon."
The 90s were eons ago,
put the scissors down, you beautiful sad bitch.

Thou shalt worship no false idols (except for Ru Paul, who, let's
face it, is as close to a representative on Earth as I've had in
roughly 2,000 years).

Thou shalt not just laugh when a male colleague says something
inappropriate,
Notice that if you were to ask Colin what exactly he means by
"nice assets," he would choke on his Tesco meal-deal sandwich
(Egg and cress, obviously, but I digress)

Thou shall feel no guilt when entering that downstairs part of
Anne Summers where they sell the vibrators,
That for some reason feels really seedy and outrageous,
Apple-flavour lube doesn't count as forbidden fruit . . .
Don't worry, I've checked.

Thou shall rebel against the space that the manspreaders
determine to introduce to our commute
Because fuck you I have legs too, you ridiculous brute,
and your claim that your genitalia really do take up that much
room, I refute

And so my children hear me now and go forth and multiply,
and divide, and subtract,
There aren't enough women in STEM, as a matter of fact
So go and smash those glass fucking ceilings
No feelings of incompetence
We are the fucking 50%
There's a reason we are known as better halves.

If these are the 10 commandments then that confirms that I am
the fucking messiah
and I can say with indefinite certainty that Ariana Grande was
right

God is a woman.

WATCHING YOU ROCK YOUR DAUGHTER TO SLEEP
Billie Partridge-Naudeer

I watch you,
Cradle her
Her Rock
You are rocking her
"Like so" you say as you hold her
"So she can get to her left thumb"
And her red-faced cries of protests they die down into slumber
I am dumbfounded when I look at you,
I see
My little baby
With her little baby
I know it's not easy
Nights spent singing those cheesy Tumble Tots nursery rhymes
But you do it with such genuine hand-on-heart joy
That the janky melodies cranked out of those toys
Sound like symphonies
And see,

You're a mother now
But you always have been
It's not lost on me,
The irony
Of my little sister wiping my tears
After nightmares,
Reassuring those fears,
Letting me curl up, in the bottom bunk, next to you.

You have always felt like home to me.
Like the warm glow of safety.
Like a pick 'n mix bag full of only the best bits,
Like the peak of a wave just before the crest tips
Into the ocean

I wanna swim where you're swimming.
And we're both just treading water but that's ok,
I'll take a deep breath to hold you up any day,
Cos I only want to win when you're winning.

And that's how she looks in your arms,
Like there's nowhere else she wants to be.
She's an extension of you and she is everything to me
I vow to protect your kin for all eternity she,

Is the sun-drenched cliffs of a new dawn,
Born on an ice-cold day she burns bright enough to forever keep
    that darkness at bay
I'd say I've never known a love like it but I have
Because it's the way
That I
Love you.

WHERE ARE YOU LITTLE GIRL?
Justine Martin

Where have you gone little girl
The wild thing with the crooked smile
Making potions out of mummy's perfume and bath water

Where are you little girl
I saw you in the mud
Drawing dreams with a stick and feeling very loved

Where are you little girl
Seeing colours in the dark
Chasing wagging tails and living out your spark

Where are you little girl
Running naked on a sandy wave so precious in your form
Something I hope you will forever save

Where are you little girl
Did you get into that car
The skies are turning grey
I hope you haven't gone far

Where are you little girl
Did you find a better place?
Somewhere where your dreams came true
And you didn't need the space

Where are you
You aren't shining very bright
I'm scared I lost you to the man who took away your light

I FLOSS MY TEETH EVERY NIGHT
Elizabeth Hadden

My mouth is a rotting thing.
An underbite tucked too tightly,
not connecting properly in some spaces.
I had braces once, but nothing could contain my tongue.

As an adult, they recommend different fixes
- reminding me that I'll stay crooked forever
if I don't push my bone around.

It's not the way my smile looks that concerns me.
My bottom teeth look like they're whispering secrets to each other,
and I miss being able to slurp noodles between my two front teeth
- a flat, starchy snake sliding between enamel.

Nothing can trap my words, and this is what scares me.

My mouth is a yelling thing
that can't be locked
behind plastic or wires.

My lower jaw hides
like an inert fist,
ready to jump.
But at night,
it attacks my tongue
closing in, clamping down
until I'm sore.

My tongue doesn't fit within my teeth,
it pokes between -
a serpent sneaking through the smile.
It has been this serpent
that's gotten me in trouble, time and time again.

My words are my downfall.
My teeth, unwilling counterparts
in a self-defeating series of events.

My mouth is a rotten thing
that cannot be reshaped
to sit straight.

UNTITLED
Lori Wallace

Contribution One
Steep me in water and submerge my seedlings
Hack my roots with an old, blunt knife
Fertilise the soil with devious whispers
Spray venom onto my leaves
Encourage sympathetic bees to an adjacent field
Let the wind carry my nectar to
Spill in a secluded creek
Twist off my flowers
Pluck each petal
Shake the stalk clean
Plant me in concrete
Let slugs consume me

WOMAN COMMITS
Maisie McGregor

I'll cage the fruit,
naked in the heartlands.

Bent backs
and desire lines

forgotten draperies
and held exits.

The ladybird on the
virginal line.

Suspended

in a starry clench.

Clenched fists
for deserved dreams
running to the space
that pinches
within thousands
of rubesque selectors.

Finished with yellow loss,
and pencils.

Commitment is within the lurch
of hand to pen

heart to brush.

MORGDEN
Maisie McGregor

She likes ragged fun
and pearlish boys
save her from frosted daylight
the night snaps
squeezing guts
and pulverising thought.

The moon's wax drops
to her hands
as it melts with her dance
- arms coiling to grasp.

The unbelted radiance
shall strike root in the night.

THE BOYS WHO NEARLY KILLED ME
Jade Angeles Fitton

What more do you want than
these white waves?
The March sun-blanched middle
of the sea.
The sand snakeskinned in patterns
by the rip currents.
Not far from where you'd find us
starting fires and drinking special brew,
right close to where you'd've found us
snoozing in the dunes.
If I keep walking with my eyes closed,
will it be over soon?

I'm not far from the
park where I got beaten up,
or the corner we took too fast
on that Honda 90cc.
I'm not too far
from the dart that only just missed me,
the bottle that nearly hit me.
On cloudy days like these,
when the cliffs are kissed with mist,
I remember with affection,
the boys who nearly killed me.

What more do you want
than a midge in the sun?
Than the branches above;
a filigree of wishbones
to crack, and whisper at –
then say, sorry, you've forgotten
what you wanted in the first place.

Not so far from the copper hope you gave
the well in Florence. When money
still had currency, and home
was still a place.

I'm not far from the bad decisions
that led that car to meet the banks.
I'm not too far from the axe he had,
the quad bike we crashed,
or the hay bales like boulders we
precariously stacked.
On cozy days like these,
when the sun comes through the window
and there's the buzz of honeybees,
I remember with affection,
the whistle of my maker
and the boys who nearly killed me.

GOOD MANNERS
Jade Angeles Fitton

Red lights start the night at 11:25 p.m. for
smoke-lit amphetamine heads,
whisky coke adrenaline, the air is wet, it drips
like rain from the collective cloud of hormonal sweat.
Long, black-coated man it's too hot to be wearing that
and I don't like the way you sidle up to me.
Move on to a friend of a friend and win, I was just a stumbling
block on your mission to keep pushing a means to an end.
Smells like someone's smoking reefer in the corner but there's
no one there.
We go outside to see if it's coming through the vents . . .

"I've done more girls than all of you.
And I'm the skinniest here, what does that mean?"
None of his friends can tell him.
He's 23 but his eyes have been punched by all the late nights
and all the laughing. I don't think he'll become a good man but
he's warm in the smoking pens outside, where foundation
and drawn-on eyebrows clash with the white of the outdoor lights.
The wind filled with men's promises
and the cackles of the gargoyles of the night.

Not far from The Alibi, and down the unloved stairs,
her lips are slit and ready for a kiss. She's smiling, and sticking
out her chest to compensate. She's self-conscious of her teeth.
I watch him clock what and who's around. What's the time Mr. Wolf?
Think it's home-time now. I catch him take a last look back
and feel sorry for his girlfriend as I watch him rub her back
as he watches me. It must be the bare skin because
we've all received that pat.
I frown. Less than I mean to because I'm half in the past.
I'm supernatural baked, girlfriend,
good luck with him.

Someone spilled my drink. You, who grinds your teeth
as the whisky sinks into my vest that was on the floor next to it.
I wouldn't say anything but my friend thinks you should buy me
another –
doubt you'll bother. I assume you'll never return,
so when you do, it's in less time than I could expect;
drawn-in
to the time-warping abilities of someone else's trip.
Gently pass the full glass, and leave like you too were once blown
apart.
From behind I see you're lined with silver,
like the washing machine your jaw could've been.
But whatever, no matter, your manners remained.

TOPANGA CANYON
Jade Angeles Fitton

There was a car over Topanga Canyon and a White Whale
Sailing through the sky, cruising down to LAX.
In the morning light
I thought I looked beautiful wrapped in a towel,
I'd have liked you to've seen it, but it's no loss of mine.

Ballets of Segway drifters floating past my sunny head,
Ukulele in the distance, meter on the mile and bacon on the side.
Bright light Pacific breeze,
A wish empties my breath and darkens my chest,
What comes in on the wind and brings me to my knees?

Miss Marianne, I heard him scream your name
40 years too late.
On Hollywood Boulevard outside a theater,
He stood there old and mad. So lost, Marianne,
Just a short cab ride from where you took the train.

Still the sun glitters the palm trees,
And artificial streams rush to calm the mildly agitated –
That's me, can't seem to shake this city breeze.
Black on black Range Rover, I watch you hurtle down the 8 lanes.
Come, bowl me over this refill of my cherry cola.

Hit the view, all's new, all's cool, all's fine.
Light another, take me to a cloud with numbers.
I've tied up my split ends and cut off all the loose ones.
There's no dead weight. Unless you count the floor to which
I am stuck,
Or you count the thoughts, of which I think of too much.

And so to bed, to my sweet dreamscape hummer,
Revving to heaven with legs of white steel.

Trash the checklist of sins. She is forgiven who forgives herself,
And she, like the space between a stepping stone and a crocodile,
Is dangerous in dreams.

PHILOSOPHY HAS ALWAYS BEEN A BOYS CLUB (WHAT I WISH I HAD BEEN TOLD AFTER FAILING INTRO TO PHILOSOPHY)

Jacqueline Moulton

Philosophy has always been a Boys Club,
surely you knew this
before you even dared to begin to think.
It's the dialectic of Kings—an elite Dead Philosophers Society.
Derrida, Man of the House, writes that as inheritors we are in
mourning & he isn't wrong for as I wring out wet from the page,
the letters & words upend, losing their shape & becoming pure
ink—ink to collect & wipe across the mouth in order to blacken
your eyes for as Nietzsche says that to get rid of God we would
need to get rid of Grammar and to get rid of Kings we would
have to get rid of Language, for Language is the game & the
whole game's rigged—no matter which way you splice it.
We inherit the concatenations of Masculinity as what is Science
as what is Truth as what is Force enough to split all the ribs,
from whence you came, open.
Slither out. Leave your skin
behind, leave your life—either
way you'll be asked to deliver
your own head to Socrates on a
platter. You won't be dining
tonight, tonight you go hungry.
Do it. Bow subserviently. Tuck
a dagger deep up your sleeve.
Swallow a match. Chase it with kerosene.
You will need these items later. Percolate.

Philosophy has always been a Boys Club.
You'll be criticized for your emotionality. Your fatal poetics.
Your rage turned manifesto only makes you a hysteric. Listen to
every critique. Let it sharpen your shiv.
Write like a sword. Swallow all

of it. Plato decries the artist for
their femininity, their propensity
to weep. This does not matter.
Weep. Think. (May they be both).
Bleed without flinching. Don't cry.
The Canon excludes you. Read it
anyway. Sharpen your teeth on it.
Cry. Read it again. Digest all that
failed Enlightenment & let your
body turn it to Shit. Disintegrate time.
Drink the marrow from the femurs of Those Who Have
Gone Before, of those who have broken their legs open, for you!
for you!
No, not for you. Do not make the mistake of lingering here too
long, here, where it is safe—for when the apocalypse comes (& to
have a word for it means it has already arrived) pull out the gold
you've hoarded & buried in your teeth & use it to gnaw your way
out of the rotting flesh you've been buried underneath. For
philosophy has always been a Boys Club but Let Me Be Clear
this metaphor is a broken one, a title gorged on itself—you've
already outlived it. Philosophy has always been a Boys Club &
this is the gift—a gift the way death is a gift. Is this fair? No. It's
a horse. Look it square in the mouth. Kiss its hooves & it will
teach you how to think on the run. Leave all this behind,
especially this poem, especially that Ivory Tower, especially all
our poor ideas about ideas, leave it.
Leave. Weep. Erect an altar.
Splint your wounds but do not let them heal.
Pull that dagger from your sleeve & with the blade held high
above your head, catching fire from the last dying light of that
desert night, you will become alighted with the mystery which
no one else knows, no one at all, not myself, not even Socrates,
even if he got close, in that moment of being sentenced to death
& drinking a poison of his own making. Decline that hemlock
cocktail.
Mix a new tincture.
Sharpen sticks.

Drive them through the heart.
Drink your own marrow.
Pierce your mind.
Slice it open.
Find it ash.
Weep.
Get back to work.
Soaked in turpentine, sit too
close to the fire. Be stuck by flint.

Let yourself burn.

Just be the one who lights the match.

DOMINION
Eleanor Perry-Smith

In a stale and tuckered outpost where we set our troubled stage
I was winded with ambition you were cloaked in restless age
And while we both knew that the answer to our riddles was the same
We departed dust and lightning reaching for that brassy ring

And all the while, for a while, all we wanted was to seem
And all we reached for was a vapor as we gathered smoke screens
And all we hunted were mirages and all we captured was the mist
Reveled in our grand delusion, all we brought home was a wish, and

In between cemented winters I heard the sneer of cruelty
So I gathered all my splinters and built a lamp by which to read, and
In the velvet light before me there's a phrase that I can see
All it says is, I believe you, I believe you, I believe

When you say that you were misled and when you wail that you
were robbed, and
When they took your amber body and burned it to their wretched
gods, and
When you know that you've been battered in ways that no one sees
It's not the skin that bears the lashing, the spirit carries that disease
When you lament there is no onward because the backward had
their way, and
When you tell me there's no justice because the judges, too, were
paid, and
When you whisper that, someday, you'll cri de cœur your own decree
By the lamplight I believe you, I believe you, I believe

So lest we forget all our saviors, let us buckle down and bleed
Be now bonded by our veins, dears, the impulse of divinity
And in the velvet light before me I saw us rise above our feet
We are nourished by the nectar of belief, dear, of belief

I don't know if there's a place in which I'll settle into peace
Since I have searched the crowded streets and found that pain is
each to each
All I know is there's a vestige of a blazing paradise
I can feel it in my backbone and see it right behind my eyes

So when we're tired from all our wanders and when the sky
becomes the ground
We'll congregate and get a pizza and get drunk on what's around
And in the velvet light before us there's a phrase we all concede
All it is, is, I believe you, I believe you, I believe

VICTORY IN RED
Casey Harloe

I bled on the street but
no one knew.
The battleground that
laid between my thighs.
No,
they would not notice
how good I felt
bleeding
beneath a white dress
in silent victory
of keeping a secret so well.
Yes,
it is a burden to hide
but it is not embarrassing.
I embrace it because
in the end
it is a beautiful thing. (Period.)

"MY STATUS QUO"
Louise King

Assess each social situation,
Anxiety delivers its own feedback,
Quietly controlling minor influence,
Simplistic friendship does not live here.

Awkward struggle finding place,
Managing on the periphery,
Unconscious acceptance, natural ease,
Missing in action completely.

Keeping up with the unconcerned,
Acceptance for the noteworthy matters,
Willingly wait as they phase you out,
Stand at the side-lines without a side.

YOUR RUT
Stacey Cotter Manière

I send out my heart to you in the form of words
you don't reply but I won't take it for love lacking.

You traverse deeper into solitude
I'm left afraid what to say
should it lead you to get lost there
and never return to me from what you call
- your rut.

I type you a letter I will never send
thoughts clouding my heart gush out at projectile speed
my fingers can't keep up, bumping into keys they should not be
touching.

I imagine I am there with you
I see your room so vividly
the light is yellowish and heavy
shadows on the wall are dark and leering
but I cannot pull you out by visualising.

We sit in your cupboard it's dark and we hold hands
fabric fibres tickle our noses and lack of air shortens our breath.
I prod you, gently, out of fear of pushing too far.

I let your heavy burdens rest on me unrequested
my heart drops heavy pulling tight on the sinew across my chest.
My lungs are restricted from breathing fresh thoughts of you
- smiling, free, light.

SEDIMENT
Amber Singh

I was born with the sediment of my mother's sorrow, I was told

My mother was 19
and 8 months belly round
when her mother died
in a suicide

So I guess you could say my mother was born with her mother's
sediment too

Murky thickness in a maternal line
our blood running black-brown
as if it already was dry on the ground

I wanted my daughter to inherit my —
and my —
but never the sediment
a dirty river is hard to carry

So I learned how to walk
with my veins open wide
a hundred eyes per capillary all hungry for the light

And then I learned how to write
with the ink of my arteries
flowing onto pages and out into pools

I learned how to swim
using only the muscles of my heart
pumping and filtering out the dark shadows of torment and rage

And I also learned how to lay
perfectly still with my ribs splayed open

so the sun could dry up the muddy riverbanks contained in
these deeps

I then learned how to fly
and convalesced with the tornados
seeking brutal winds to howl the remnants right out of me

Oh and then I learned how to love
from the contributions and transfusions offered by
the good-hearted people of my local blood bank

One day I cut myself open and
held my own me up to find
blood that was

Bright and
Light and
Right and

So then finally I learned how to grow a tiny human
out of a sesame seed
and then we were two hearts beating and dreaming in this true
red blood

And what to do when two bodies are beating bright blood
in rhythm and in tune
but laugh?

So we laughed
and laughed
right down in the echo of veins where a Ganges river of sadness
had once been

I laughed so hard
my water broke
a happy ocean tide that all the rivers flowed to

And my perfect daughter
came rushing out
to stamp out
the collective sorrow of a whole
maternal line
with one pure inky newborn foot
pressed on cream hospital paper

FOR HER
Sorcha Collister

Do it for yourself
Do you?
Who's it all for -

She buys bags, paints nails
For her,
The shoes, their red sole, hers.

But, the eyes, are his
The curves,
Her fire, red soul, for him.

To have and to hold,
Occupy,
Possess and reserve.

The body, the skin,
Those eyes
And these curves,

All she truly owns,
Does not belong to her.
He asked once nicely -

Borrowed on high interest,
I repeat, no return,
Taxed on the street, credit loss, my concern.

Alcohol, sugar,
Spare bedroom, tax,
Bureaucratic, executive, governing her dance.

He supervises her submission,

Regulates her gesticulates,
Presides her demise.

He is, in control,
Let the pendulum swing,
This cyclical life.

Let gravity hold it down,
Firm this time,
Let's play fair, get even, let it all be
                                        - mine.

GROWING THROUGH WHISTLES IN THE WIND
Sorcha Collister

Don't drag your feet
Through tiring years
You'll wear through your sweet souls

    Pick up, step forward strut

Such pretty eyes
For stolen looks
Stray gaze hangs in the air

    She blinks, she winks, she cries

You forgot to smile
On weary days
A waste of clenched teeth

    Chin up, turn, 'round those corners

Wearing sacks
Her hidden figure
Put on your fancy clothes

    Her curves, swerves and figurines

Left wondering
What fix to make
Frown lines less travelled by

    Smiles, bags, make all the difference

Improving's fine
But sighs, comments

And a wolf's remarks

Are as strong as whistles in the wind.

TOAST FOR DINNER
Georgie Jesson

Whatever selfish beauty coursed through your veins
Now charges through mine
By virtue of blood and guilt
And you would always cry, and so do I.

Memory of you is a pink ribbon,
A tape spooling forwards to recover the past
Even after death you are recovering still
I watch you roll the rock through the tinted glass.

You had lost a few days,
One being my birthday
Life paid you a pittance
You paid me a crumpled up fiver bouncing back to life
In my puffed up porcelain hands
And with all the respect I knew
I gave it back to you
Knowing I did not need it more than you.

That was a memory.
Driving a little red car along the tracks
Of your arms
These are my memories.
Sucking the nicotine out of my hair
My memories.
Toast for dinner
What can that possibly mean to anyone but me?

I thought you gave up too soon
They said you left it too late
But no! Grief is not a cliché –
And the beautiful gift you have given me is the strength to
control the tape.

You taught me that life is violent
And now I love with that violence
I see the suffering in suffering
I feel the silence in silence.

LEGACY
Miranda Gold

Dim. Blink of an eye cracks.
A hair-line in the shell blind.
See even this Nothing
has shades – the shade
of a lid opened – shiver
open in this quiet light
after candlelight.
First Knowledge
given, taken,
night in, night out
lights out.

"Are you awake?"

Only at the door can you tell
new shades from old,
leave your name behind –

"Are you awake?"

They forgot to remember to forget
their names their words their worlds.
So you make their worlds in words
to feed a myth of your own making
made from that echo *Unspeakable* –
that empty *Unspeakable* –
and make so much Nothing
from nothing till we reach
again the quiet light
after candlelight.
Touch again
the weight -

Unspeakable

"Are you awake?"

- but your myth has no need for words not now.
Ulcers write legacies of a body humiliated
hearing your father turn and turn -
you hear what bones say
hear the memory of bones:
bones fine lace edging the cloth
in the quiet light of candlelight.
Unattended. Automatic
we stand pray sit -

"Are you awake?"

chew and swallow the *Unspeakable*
assimilating the language of moans and gasps.
All in the gentleness of the quiet light of candlelight.
Engorged shadows pour the Nothing ladled
out, out – you had to get out
because they had to get out
and couldn't get out –

"Are you awake?"

cut out smiles and papery laughs - a paper chain
from him to you to me caught by the quiet light
the gentle light of candlelight.
Footsteps back up the stairs -
you cannot stay for the blink
the shiver and the eye
looking back through yours to his:
the Nothing that is everything that must be brought back
from that place beyond words – if we let *Unspeakable*
make its claim, you will always be at my door –

"Are you awake?"

TEXTING THE TEENAGE SELF
Golnoosh Nourpanah

your mother called
      you a slut:
Sexually transmitted distrust
Lust, and never love
Urban because you're urban as in trapped in the steely structure
of cities
Tame which U weren't but wish U had been
and T for terrible trouble tomb tarnish
and T for take which you do
and taken which you are
but truth is T is for trapped
because that's the only state you felt when you
were called a slut by your
Mum, your siblings, your dates
even your cakes. When you opened your mouth to gulp
them, they flashed their teeth
and called you a
Sexpest
Loveless
Umbilical
Taboo
tolerated only by dark chocolate, not even cakes
by muddy tea, expired milk, rotten cheese
U eat and spit and swallow and escape
and cover your ears but can still hear what
U are

S.L.U.T.

Salute to you to your evergreen lust, and your blood
Loss and blood clots in your breakfast
U can do better, you could have committed
      and performed and you could have digested instead of

swallow like an arrowed sparrow, you run and
Take take take and you could not explain to your mother or
      to yourself that there was a ray, an energy in their flashing flesh
      and glittery eyes that made you grant them what they requested
so you flew from the city of your virginity to a garden infested with
flowers
you stared picked sniffed until you were a peacock not a teenage stench
      and it is true U are not
tame, and that's O.K. and thou shalt not be taken.

BASTARD
Golnoosh Nourpanah

I forgot about him until he came to me in a dream:
on a hazy beach in a blue bikini, his lips, plump and crimson.
The first time I met him, I was a dizzy virgin, eighteen,
and all I wanted was to be admired
by an older lecturer who looked as young as me.
Years later, in another country,
far from our flames, he comes back to me in a bikini, in blood
lipstick
not saying anything, just gazing, small eyes squinting from
behind enormous glasses,
the eternal barrier between his skin and mine.
He always wore boring clothes, black and mustard yellow
but my dream queered him.
Did he ever want me? Sniffing my sour perfume in his sunlit
office, he did not touch me. His elegant hands, my ivory plants
caressed against my fingers twice, exchanging
Coetzee's *Disgrace*. Later he texted me in English
keep it as a present felt like an insult between my teenage legs
I assumed he did not want to end up like that professor
who was obsessed with Byron and slept with his student,
and subsequently was fired and his daughter got raped.
But my love was in love with linguistics.
He did not sleep with me
he deconstructed deconstruction so much so
that even I got bored
I opened my legs beneath my black hijab
convinced that he could see everything, and nobody
else could see anything. At the age of eighteen one is
convinced one can drink anything one desires,
even if that desire is married with two kids.
But I did not want to be fucked. And neither did he.
What were our nervous surreptitions about?

Twelve years later:
As I sit behind my teacherly desk
discussing deconstruction,
I find myself mimicking him.
And in my dream, I have an epiphany:
I never desired him. I desired to be him. To shield behind
a desk, skimming students like a cat staring
at rats, and spitting, "Foucault says every piece of art is a
bastard."

DUST
Amy Burgwin

Some time later I slip in
through the usual veil
and into the trembles of a dream.

It is not the past but a place coated with dust
as weightless as a mist, as delicate as peach silk,
I cannot touch what is as dainty as a spider's web.
A clearing of a throat will dissolve it.
It is all lavender here.

I cannot walk around in this world.
It is set to the same three bars of a song,
a reverb, a prolonged echoing second.
There is a clock tower, out of frame
and this whole thing lives in its looping chimes.

Silvery hair, she brushes it stiffly
the candlelight warms her dead face.
Around her are the relics; jewels, old clocks,
and through somebody's nostalgia
I come to shimmering sadness, peaking decay.

I think there is a laughing track playing softly
and a hum, the end of a record, somewhere.
This place is still and macabre,
not as fluid as a dream or as flawed as life.
I have tried to get here.

      (with tinny war-time songs
      discarded Victorian tintypes
      soiled, disintegrating dress linings
      two-minute musical intros
      buzzing static)

It is not the past, but a place coated with dust,
the dust left behind by the moving present
                              coated with death.
No one knows of this place except me
because only the dead are still here and they are locked in it
              automatons, scripted people.
This world is a show reel of a moment.

I have always wanted to become a ghost story.
I slip in, eventually.

MAIDEN, MOTHER, CRONE REVERSED
Julia Houghton

She had always felt more crone than maiden.
Innocence was never easy for her.
Impulse pushed,
pulled and propelled her to the wild.
She did not resist temptations.

She thought the maiden dead within.
She gave herself with relished freedom.
Consumed by what others called sin.
Not obligated to anybody's regulations.

Threats and punishment loomed,
but the dogma did not call to her
as it did to other people.
Confused by each sensation.

Until a calling came from something deeper.
A primal paganism of the heart.
Washing wild waves through the whole of her being and growing
belly.

At last she looked upon the misunderstood maiden that she never
thought had been there.
She held her breath and laid to rest
the past that the ragged maiden made.

On her ripest day she believed the goddess came to watch.
Not visible to the eye
as she never is,
but she felt her as if she were her own skin. Her own flesh.
She sensed her in the flowing of joint blood.

Whispered words of wild wonder.

As the burning of new life burst forth.
With one first breath she turned from mortal lead to eternal
levitating lava.

Someday she may miss that hidden maiden that she hardly felt
she'd known.
(The one that you stole)
The folly.
The dangerous tendency to roam.

These moments are just fleeting,
as I now see you dreaming,
and I watch that maiden born again in you.

Change circles in our cells from birth, creates us anew daily.
Death is life and life is death.
We are the seasons ever changing.
We are all the testament to womanhood
that they could never burn away.

I'll watch you grow.
In hope to become a crone,
that will see you a maiden then a mother born.

I never thought a trinity was meant for me.
Reversed it revealed itself quite neatly.
Now I find that whispered prophecy
echo in each breath,
each smile,
each day of gifted existence.

So I'll give my thanks.
Not in church prayer,
but by living each day
knowing this life has meaning because it gave me you.

FIRST KISS
Monica Medeiros

There's the first kiss
I tell of
appropriate, cute
but it was the second.
It's not entirely my fault
I lie.
Messy details
are uncomfortable.
One is constantly perched
on consideration.

She was watching *My Little Pony*.
He was part of grown-up people.
She smiled when she watched
the colourful ponies, but
she felt he
watched her watching.
He moved her little body
so it wasn't hers anymore.
Suddenly,
there was flesh in her,
the slithering tongue
pulsing huge, pushing in and out.
It was wet. A hard mouth-
full of tissue,
raw and unformed.
She wanted to stop the sensation
of falling.
She heard keys jar
against the door
and returned
momentarily.
She thought people could see

it on her,
that she stunk of it, the act.
The moisture that pooled at the
corners of her lips
stayed permanent.
Years passed until she saw him,
in public
and she was ready
for the indiscretion. The enormity
of it. To reclaim
her mouth was ripe and ready
but when she tried
it filled up and she choked
on the mad dash
of wild, little ponies.

THIS BODY
Sarah-Jane Lovett

This body is a trojan,
It's a vestal being
A crazy machine
taken for granted.
It is criticised for some
wrong lines, or bumps
or even mere proportions.
Tough.
This is a dynamo of a body
which has been a precocious
child
and birthed a child or two.
It is a strange little baby place,
with a cool little swimming pool onboard.
A body that can swim like a fish and a fiend,
and just row on through life's salty tears
and whip up a white cloud of a meringue
to just lose yourself in.

This body can deftly wipe
a small button nose and
can clean and bandage a hurt leg.
It has helped to bury the darling mother,
and knelt by the side of
the failing family dog.
It has loved a wrong 'un
and taken a tumble with a right one
and fallen up and down
Alice-like
in life
and back again with gusto.

It can carry all the shopping

to make a whopping feast.
How long have you got?
This body sometimes gets a sore knee,
the occasional little ache.
The birth passage should not be up for
assessment, however one feels.
Breasts that have fed babies
are not there for the "pencil pertness"
test
Oh no.
And all discussion of what sort of nick it's all in.
Stop it with the cellulite.
This body is a goddam work
in progress,
Picasso; cubist phase, since you ask.
It may be shot to pieces in places
So say wear and tear if you dare
no matter, a little fatter
clothed or bare
if you dare.
So give it up for your big life quilt,
Forget about tiny marks, or small lines
and think of fine wines.
A soupcon instead
of Chateau Lafite
as a treat,
and give thanks
to
and
for
your body.

I AM A STORM
Roosa Herranen

There are oceans in my eyes
and my mind is a storm
Flirting is an art form
I'm easily painted as cheap
I just need the uniform
I know, you know it
You are vulnerable
Uncomfortable
You can't quite pin me down
Literally or metaphorically
I am "too much" and you keep saying that
But what does "intimidating" even mean?
Talk dirty to me and throw me away
I was never going to stay

POLLUTION
Roosa Herranen

The strong, witty female I am
does not hear your words
Your judgmental thoughts
that you're spreading around
have no value at all because I will be renowned for speaking up my mind
I have no reason to hide
and I will fight
against your pollution that is trying to dim my light
This light that will blind your
ignorant eyes
I am a strong, witty female
I am never defined by what you see me as
I am my own
Woman!
You are yours
I am a strong, witty female
I do not hear your words

THE NIGHT MY MOTHER DIED
Barbara Polla

The night my mother died
She looked at me so seriously
I should have understood
That's not what she wanted

Not morphine
Not this waiting
No last sigh
Although there were three of them

The night my mother died
I should have called Murat
Long before these three sighs
And have him play bouzouk

And have him play kanoun
All night long
My mother loved the music
And she would love Murat

She loved beautiful men
Loved the music and
Freedom
And singing all along

The night my mother died
Something died in me
I would prefer not to
Be there in family

So I called Murat
And he brought his bouzouk
And brought his kanoun

And his beauty and his voice

And he sang all night long
And I danced on the terrace
For the life she gave me
For the joy and the music

And she went her own way
With Murat in her eyes
With the music in her ears
The night my mother died

We weren't serious at all
The stars pulled down for real
The icebergs melted down
And the music was so loud

That none of us heard these three sighs
Not even her
The dying angel
And the next morning

When they came to get her
The morticians
I didn't feel to flee
Murat's music took my hand

Paved the way
Closed my eyes
Freed my tears
She was gone

UNNAMED 1,2,3,4,5,6
Elle En Kay

masking the deterioration
for the seeds planted within are
constrained by the everlasting
awe of basking in a bliss
that was laced by the
frost of death
— Elle En Kay

washed upon the brink
of hope and the lust
for an invisible
craving — tell me
alas where the
memories are
hidden?
i'll bask awaiting at
the shore for
the breeze
carries your scent
— Elle En Kay

i'll believe the subtleties
as such/as such/as
only such as/you
seduced thy mind #2
allow a rope to
form in which
I am left me
only one tugging
— Elle En Kay

in the depths of crass,
we met laced with
a sense of fragility
upon which our sense
of touch soon melted
away any and all
~~sense of~~
being

—Elle En Kay

I'll meet you in the dream
after next - in the whisks
of darkness, we will weep.
I'll meet you in the time
after next - in the silence
of space, we will mourn.
I'll meet you in a moment
for our breaths
are entangled.

—Elle En Kay

They say the sea drifts
upon shattered glass
blended in with
lost love letters
but to think of
the blood dripping
as words is
oh so / oh so
oh so
quivering to our
very own
existence

—Elle En Kay